insight text guide

Scott Hurley

Things Fall Apart

Chinua Achebe

insight™

innovative engaging evolving

First published in 2001, reprinted with minor amendments in 2019.

Insight Publications Pty Ltd
3/350 Charman Road
Cheltenham VIC 3192
Australia
Tel: +61 3 8571 4950
Fax: +61 3 8571 0257
Email: books@insightpublications.com.au

www.insightpublications.com.au

A catalogue record for this book is available from the National Library of Australia

Chinua Achebe's Things Fall Apart / Scott Hurley

ISBNs:
9781875882755 (print)
9781925778731 (digital)
9781925778748 (bundle: print + digital)

Cover design by Gisela Beer, based on a concept by The Modern Art Production Group

Printed by Markono Print Media Pte Ltd

contents

CHARACTER MAP

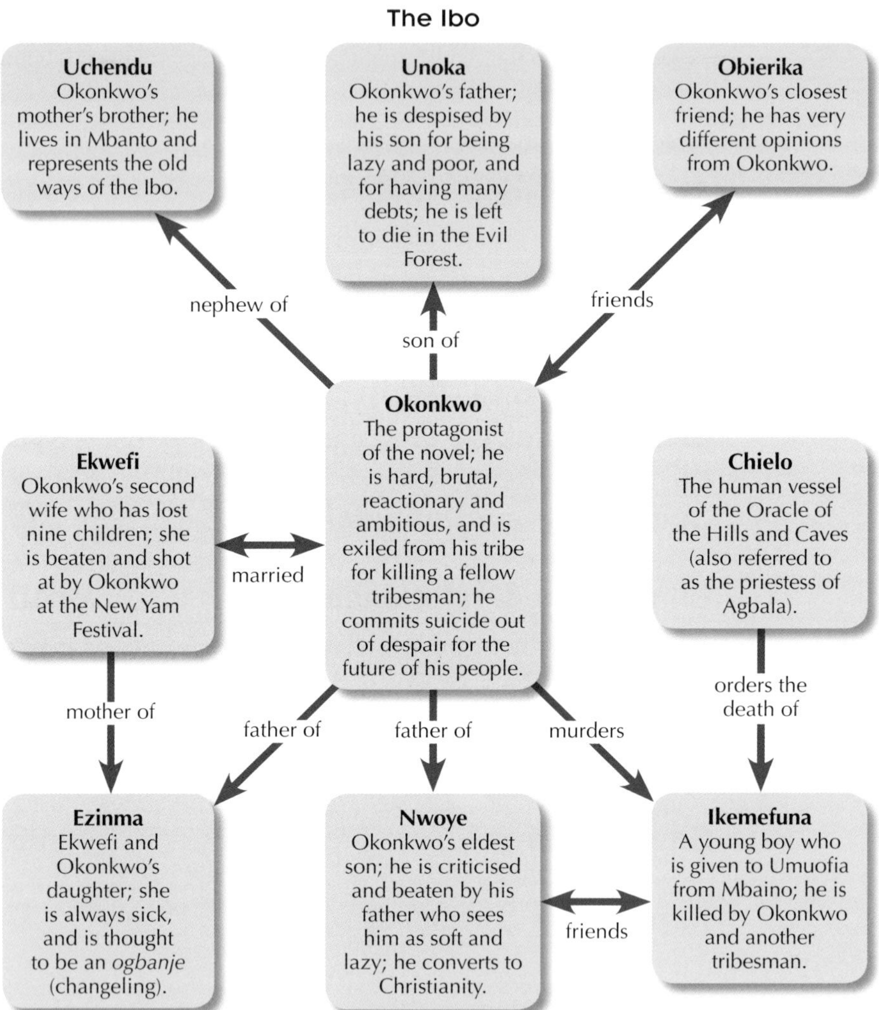

British Empire / White colonisers

Mr Brown
First white missionary to attempt to convert the Ibo to Christianity; he uses subtle means of manipulation.

Mr Smith
White missionary who replaces Mr Brown; he is an aggressive zealot.

The District Commissioner
A representative of British colonial rule; he abuses the British system of 'justice' to control the Ibo.

INTRODUCTION

Things Fall Apart, originally published in 1958, is Chinua Achebe's first novel. Born in 1930 in Ogidi, Nigeria, Achebe was one of the first graduates of the University College of Ibadan. *Things Fall Apart* is one of the world's best-known novels; it has been translated from English into over fifty languages and has sold more than twenty million copies worldwide.

Regarded as the 'father of modern African literature' (an endorsement that Achebe himself rejected), Achebe wrote *Things Fall Apart* to begin dismantling the way Africans were represented to the world in such works as Joseph Conrad's *The Heart of Darkness* and Joyce Cary's *Mister Johnson*. These and other European works (not only novels but also poetry, drama and, most notably, anthropological treatises and histories) portrayed Africans as primitive, mysterious, violent, unpredictable or childlike, contributing to the justification of the violent – and profitable – colonisation of the so-called Dark Continent by 'enlightened' Europeans. *Things Fall Apart* is an important Nigerian novel; it is one of the first written in English to look at Africa from the perspective of Africans, rather than through the eyes of Europeans. Believing that the way a culture represents itself is through its stories, Achebe gives voice to the stories of his people, the Ibo of Nigeria, at the time of their colonisation by the British late in the nineteenth century.

The publishing of this novel was like the opening of a floodgate. Since 1958 a vast wealth of literature has emerged by writers from all over the African continent. Some of the most notable of these authors include Ayi Kwei Armah, Ngũgĩ wa Thiong'o and Chimamanda Ngozi Adichie, whose novel *Purple Hibiscus* (2003) was nominated for a Booker Prize. Achebe himself wrote four other novels after the publication of *Things Fall Apart*, as well as books of poetry and essays. He spent the final years of his life in the United States but was buried in 2013 in Nigeria, a nation that in 1999 witnessed its first democratically elected president after sixteen years of crippling dictatorships. In an interview with *The Atlantic Monthly* in 2000, Achebe expressed his hope that the world of the twenty-first century would see 'a balance of stories where every people will be able to contribute to a definition of themselves, where [they] are not victims of other people's accounts' (Bacon 2000).

Things Fall Apart explores the rich culture of the Ibo – its religion, folklore, ritual and political structures – through the story of Okonkwo and his family towards the end of the nineteenth century. Okonkwo is a fierce man, motivated to violence and cruelty by his persistent fears of failure and weakness. Though it is difficult to like Okonkwo during much of the novel, the reader comes to identify with him when the world of the Ibo is changed utterly by the incursion of British missionaries and the colonial civil government supporting them. Okonkwo's fatal antipathy to the British comes to represent the heroic but doomed resistance of indigenous peoples to those who would colonise them both physically and culturally.

BACKGROUND & CONTEXT

Nigeria's people

Nigeria, Africa's most heavily populated country, is incredibly diverse. It is home to more than 250 ethnic groups with their own languages and customs. Ten of these groups – the Hausa, Yoruba, Ibo, Ibibio, Fulani, Tiv, Kanuri, Ijo, Nupe and Edo – comprise nine-tenths of the population, with the first three being the largest ethnic groups. The Ibo have traditionally inhabited the southeast part of Nigeria, called Igboland or, sometimes, Iboland. (In the novel the people and their language are both referred to as 'Ibo'. 'Igbo' is now the accepted spelling for both.) In the 1960s, after local Hausa massacred between 10 000 and 30 000 Ibo in the Northern Region, the remaining Ibo fled to their traditional homeland. The Ibo declared the Eastern Region as the independent nation of Biafra in May 1967 and most non-Ibo were expelled from the region. After an intense war with a Nigerian government that refused to recognise the nation – a war marked by the death of possibly millions of people through starvation – Biafra ceased to exist in January 1970. Since then, the Ibo have remained one of the largest of Nigeria's ethnic groups.

Nigeria becomes a British colony

Europeans first reached Nigeria as early as the fifteenth century. The Portuguese began the slave trade that flourished along the West Coast of Africa until well into the nineteenth century. However, very little incursion was made into what is called the Nigerian hinterland, where the Ibo live, in the region of the lower Niger River. This explains the Ibos' almost complete ignorance of European settlers until one actually appears in the town of Abame during the time of Okonkwo's seven-year exile in the village of Mbanto. The British, who had abolished slave trading in 1807, established themselves as quasi-protectors of the area against nations that continued to trade in slaves. Before long, the British became the main power in the region, formerly annexing Lagos (Nigeria's largest city) in 1861 and capitalising on its valuable palm oil trade. Nigeria became a separate British colony in 1886, incorporating all its territory in the area, with its many diverse ethnic nations, into one entity. Not long after, missionaries began to bring Christianity into the previously isolated areas of the colony. *Things Fall Apart* is set within this period and depicts as its primary focus the subsequent conflict of cultures.

Nigeria gains its independence

It was not until 1960, two years after *Things Fall Apart* was published, that Nigeria gained its independence and became a member of the Commonwealth and the United Nations. This was the period when most of the old European colonies began, after many years of agitating for independence, to become the emerging nations of Africa; however, this was by no means a simple process. Nigeria was subject to terrible ethnic tensions (as in the conflict over Biafra), as well as the self-serving regimes of a series of dictators. These problems are in many ways attributable to the legacy of the British and the arbitrary creation of a single nation from very different ethnic groups that had had virtually no contact with one another until colonisation.

Before pulling out, the British groomed a small intellectual elite to govern Nigeria after independence. From this group have emerged leaders more interested in lining their own pockets than advancing the nation. (It should be noted that Nigeria is a country of enormous potential wealth; it has one-third of all of Africa's oil supplies and about the same portion of its natural gas reserves.) Perhaps the worst of Nigeria's leaders was the military dictator Sani Abacha, who came to power in 1993. He died in 1998, but not before robbing the country of billions of dollars and allowing the nation's reasonably adequate infrastructure to collapse. With Olusegun Obasanjo's ascension to the presidency in 1999, Nigeria once again had a democratically elected government. This has continued under his successors, Umaru Musa Yar'Adua, Goodluck Jonathan and Muhammadu Buhari.

Postcolonialism

'Postcolonial' means occurring or existing after the end of colonial rule. A colony is a country, territory or region settled by people from another country, whether or not the area is already inhabited. The settlers or colonisers are controlled by leaders from their own country (known as the mother or home country). Colonial policies have come under close scrutiny since the 1970s, with colonisers criticised for the economic exploitation of indigenous peoples. Most colonisers have since returned rule of these countries to the inhabitants of the colonised land (though not necessarily to the indigenous people). As a result, we are now in a postcolonial era.

Postcolonialism is a field of literary and cultural criticism that has only emerged in the past fifty years or so. *Things Fall Apart* is considered to be one of the foundational works of postcolonial literature. In brief, postcolonialism is a way of interpreting the literature of or about nations once subject to European colonisation. It analyses these texts in terms of how they have responded to or have been conditioned by the colonial experience. Postcolonialism means many different things to different people; part of this is due to the sheer enormity of the colonial enterprise. Those nations once colonised cover vast areas of the globe and represent incredibly different cultures; therefore, it is improbable that there could be a *single* theoretical approach for understanding and discussing the ways in which the literature of these countries describe the experiences of colonisation and its aftermath.

However, certain basic ideas, as described on the following pages, have become more or less 'standard' concepts of postcolonialism.

Postcolonial literature:

- questions and dismantles Western attitudes to colonised nations and peoples – these attitudes are described as being 'Eurocentric' (i.e. centred on European values)
- offers an alternative history (one from the perspective of the colonised subject) to that presented from the Eurocentric perspective
- attempts to bring to the centre of international cultural consciousness experiences, histories and art that have until now been marginal
- questions the assumption that the colonised nations should aspire to Western values
- undertakes to expose the fundamental racism inherent in the relationship between colonisers and the colonised
- is as interested in the legacy of colonialism as it is in colonialism itself – this legacy is evident in the state (psychological, economic or political) of the colonised nation or people after the coloniser has gone.

Postcolonial criticism:

- examines the above features in the literature of postcolonial nations, and their presence, or absence, in the Western literary canon (i.e. the body of texts thought to be of great literary merit)
- explores the way canonical Western literature can reinforce the racist or cultural stereotypes associated with colonialism.

Postcolonial literature and criticism examine:

- how once-colonised nations create different identities for themselves after the period of colonisation
- the ways that the education system and the language of the colonising nation have altered the culture of the colonised nation – this topic is of particular interest considering how much postcolonial literature (*Things Fall Apart* included) is written in the language of the coloniser
- how the colonial experience has affected the functions of race, gender and class for both the coloniser and the colonised.

Not all of the aforementioned points are necessarily applicable to *Things Fall Apart*. The particular ways in which the novel is postcolonial are listed below. (See also 'Themes, ideas & values' on page 52 for further discussion of Achebe's novel as an example of postcolonial literature.)

- It offers an alternative (here, the Ibo version) to the history of the British colonisation of Nigeria.
- It explores the Ibo culture thoroughly enough to dismantle Eurocentric perceptions of it.
- It gives the Ibo their 'story', and thus finds a way to allow them 'to contribute to a definition of themselves' (Bacon 2000).

Some critical approaches to the book almost ignore the first part of the novel, about Okonkwo's life and the practices of the Ibo before white men enter their world. While the lasting importance to some critics may be the way Achebe handles the confrontation between the colonisers and the native people, the depiction of the life and culture of the Ibo before colonisation is equally important. Achebe adopts the postcolonial cause primarily by giving voice to the stories of his people and by showing how rich their culture was before being forever changed by the incursion of the British.

The title

Achebe takes his title from one of the twentieth century's most famous poems: 'The Second Coming', by Irish poet William Butler Yeats. Much has been made of this choice, but not necessarily to a useful end. In an interview for *The Paris Review* Achebe said, 'I wouldn't make too much of that. I was showing off more than anything else' (Brooks 1994). Still, there is much in Yeats' astonishing poem that lends itself to the themes of Achebe's novel, particularly those concerning chaos and the destruction of all that made sense in the world of the Ibo before the coming of the British. You might consider other possible connections to this poem, shown on the following page, while reading *Things Fall Apart*.

The Second Coming (1920)

Turning and turning in the widening gyre
The falcon cannot hear the falconer;
Things fall apart; the centre cannot hold;
Mere anarchy is loosed upon the world,
The blood-dimmed tide is loosed, and everywhere
The ceremony of innocence is drowned;
The best lack all conviction, while the worst
Are full of passionate intensity.

Surely some revelation is at hand;
Surely the Second Coming is at hand;
The Second Coming! Hardly are those words out
When a vast image out of Spiritus Mundi
Troubles my sight: somewhere in sands of the desert
A shape with lion body and the head of a man,
A gaze blank and pitiless as the sun,
Is moving its slow thighs, while all about it
Reel shadows of the indignant desert birds.
The darkness drops again; but now I know
That twenty centuries of stony sleep
Were vexed to nightmare by a rocking cradle,
And what rough beast, its hour come round at last
Slouches towards Bethlehem to be born?

GENRE, STRUCTURE & STYLE

The novel form and the use of English

Achebe's choice of genre also enters the postcolonial discussion, for better or for worse. The novel form was born and bred in Europe (in fact, it came into life very soon after the inception of European colonialism). Some critics, associating the genre with Eurocentrism, question whether authors writing against colonialism should even use the novel as a means of expression. A more appropriate question to pose, however, relates to the discussion about language. The great majority of postcolonial literature is, of course, written in the language of the coloniser – English in Achebe's case (indeed, the great majority of *all* postcolonial literature is written in English).

Language is recognised as one of the most powerful tools in colonisation. One of the first things colonial powers do is install their language as the language of commerce, education, law etc. This means that the colonised subjects must learn this new language in order to participate in politics, work and government. Their own language takes on negative connotations, if it is not suppressed outright, and becomes detached from the practical aspects of life. Two things then occur: first, the colonised subjects, having to communicate in a language not their own, are deemed primitive, unintelligent and uncivilised; and second, deprived of their own language, the colonised subjects begin to lose the most fundamental connection to their own culture and history.

Should postcolonial writers use the novel form?

Let us consider the argument that postcolonial authors should not use the form of the novel. To begin with, the novel has become the dominant literary form in a relatively short time for a very simple reason: it is incredibly flexible. Denying oneself the use of this tool, for whatever reason, would be to severely limit one's means of expression. The whole world reads novels – many people have never read, and will never read, a piece of creative writing that is *not* a novel. As pointed out previously, one of the aims of postcolonialism is to bring marginal cultures into the centre of international cultural consciousness. The novel is the most effective literary format through which this can be achieved because of its popularity.

Choice of language

Many authors associated with postcolonialism see English as one of a writer's greatest weapons against the prejudices of colonialism. To master the language of the colonisers and use it against the colonial system is to destroy one of the fundamental justifications for the practice in the first place: that the colonised subjects are inferior, primitive and uneducable. If Achebe wrote his novel in his particular dialect of Ibo (there is a Standard Ibo, but Achebe does not speak it), how many people would have read it and continued to read it? There is a sad irony to the fact that Ibo – the language and culture the novel champions – is not one of the many languages in which *Things Fall Apart* has been published. But as Achebe says in an interview for *The Atlantic Monthly*:

> In the logic of colonization and decolonization, [English] is actually a very powerful weapon in the fight to regain what was yours. English was the language of colonization itself. It is not simply something you use because you have it anyway; it is something which you can actively claim to use as an effective weapon, as a counter argument to colonization. (Bacon 2000)

Structure

The novel has three parts. The first and longest covers the period before Okonkwo's exile to Mbanta. Though there are some allusions to the past – in Okonkwo's memories of his first year planting yams or of his father Unoka – Part One covers a little more than three years, from the arrival of Ikemefuna to the fateful funeral ceremony at which Okonkwo accidentally kills one of the mourners. Part Two is about one-third the length of Part One, but it covers the seven years of Okonkwo's exile. Part Three, the same length as Part Two, covers the very short period between Okonkwo's return to Umuofia and his death.

The conflict that dominates the political reading of *Things Fall Apart*, the one between the Ibo and the British, only begins towards the end of Part Two. Part One is about the Ibo alone. This section contains most of the observations of Ibo culture, including the funeral and marriage customs; the importance of the ancestors and the gods, as represented by the Oracle of the Hills and Caves; the ceremonies of the kola nut and the use of palm wine; and the many observations of the domestic sphere.

Style

For an author who has become famous as a founder of postcolonial literature, Achebe makes very few judgements in *Things Fall Apart*, either about the British or the Ibo. This is perhaps *why* the novel has been so influential. While Achebe's style is not necessarily journalistic (a typically dry kind of writing compared to Achebe's expressive prose), he does report things 'as they were', without any kind of leading or judgemental language. He writes about Unoka's love for music with the same kind of detached observation that he employs for the killing of Ikemefuna. This seems very important in representing the Ibo fairly. In tone, Achebe neither advocates nor denigrates. His objectives are honesty and clarity.

This makes for very effective storytelling. By the time the white men come, the reader has reached their own conclusions about what impact these colonisers will have on the Ibo culture. Achebe does not lead us one way or the other; nor does he need to. His neutral style also serves an important function in postcolonial terms. Achebe's primary goal in that regard is to give voice back to the Ibo. This requires dismantling the Eurocentric ideas about these and other native peoples that may reside in the minds of his readers. Such perceptions tend to fall into one of two extremes: either the culture is deemed to be 'savage', or to have a pristine innocence. Either one leads to a judgement of the culture as 'primitive' – childlike and unsophisticated. In postcolonial terms, such thinking is called 'mystification'. Once a different culture is 'mystified' (seen as something completely different or 'exotic', and at a lower level on some quasi-evolutionary scale) it becomes easy to justify colonising it. Part of the project of the postcolonial writer is to demystify the colonised culture. Achebe's neutral and unsentimental style allows the complexity of the Ibo culture to show through, unaffected by Western prejudices about the 'exotic' or the 'savage' or the 'primitive'.

Achebe's style is anecdotal, just as his plot is episodic. One of the most admirable things about the novel is how Achebe intertwines the story about Okonkwo with his almost anthropological representation of the Ibo culture. The observations that belong to the latter are always attached somehow to important aspects of the plot itself. For example, in Chapter 13, Achebe's close descriptions of the procedures of an Ibo warrior's funeral merge with the story of Okonkwo's banishment, brought about by the accidental death in the midst of the ritual.

SECTION-BY-SECTION ANALYSIS

PART ONE

Chapter 1 (pp.3–8)

Summary: *The main character, Okonkwo, is introduced, as is his father, Unoka, whom Okonkwo hates.*

Achebe begins his novel with the anecdote about Okonkwo throwing Amalinze the Cat. This little episode introduces the reader, better than any conventional description could, to the central characteristics of Okonkwo's personality: violence and ambition. We learn that after his victory at wrestling, his 'fame had grown like a bush-fire' (p.3) in the dry Saharan wind. Okonkwo's terrible temper is also described here.

In contrast to Okonkwo is his deceased father, Unoka, an 'unsuccessful' man, the type that Okonkwo 'had no patience with' (p.4). Unoka is described as 'lazy and improvident' (p.4) – not particularly positive characteristics, it is true, but Unoka is anything but a negative character. He believes in living for the day, in eating 'what one had in one's lifetime' (p.4). He is fond of music and conversation, a lover of beauty able to find it in the most common things, such as a sunrise or the return of the kites during the dry season. It is true that Unoka is a debtor, and that people make fun of him for it – but people continue to lend him money, their mistrust dispelled, no doubt, by his good humour and joy for life.

Q What is the significance of the character differences between Okonkwo and his father?

Chapter 2 (pp.9–15)

Summary: *A woman of Umuofia is murdered in Mbaino; Okonkwo is dispatched there to demand reparations.*

Achebe never misses an opportunity to teach his readers about the ways of the Ibo as he tells his story. Here we learn about the Ibo superstition surrounding the kind of moonless night upon which the news arrives that 'a daughter of Umuofia' (p.11) has been murdered in the village of Mbaino. War seems imminent, but surprisingly, there are formal procedures for such a terrible occurrence: Umuofia will demand 'a young man and a virgin as compensation' (p.11).

We learn that neighbouring clans fear Umuofia because of its strong medicine in war. This medicine takes the physical form of an old woman called *agadi-nwayi*. In fear of this medicine, Mbaino cooperates to avoid war, allowing Okonkwo, who has been sent as an 'emissary of war' (p.12), to return home with a young woman and a boy named Ikemefuna. The former is given to Ogbuefi Udo to replace his murdered wife. After some deliberation it is decided that Ikemefuna will stay in Okonkwo's compound until it is decided what to do with him.

Continuing the psychological profile of his protagonist, Achebe tells us that the course of Okonkwo's life has been plotted by the fear of seeming weak and ineffectual. Having heard another child refer to his father as *agbala*, an Ibo term referring both to 'woman' and the kind of man who does not take a title, Okonkwo vows that it shall never be applied to him. This creates industriousness, but also cruelty. Okonkwo rules his household 'with a heavy hand' (p.12). He has three wives and numerous children who inhabit separate huts within his compound; however, most of his cruelty is aimed at his oldest son, the twelve-year-old Nwoye, in whom he thinks he already recognises some of his father Unoka's characteristics.

Q Why do you think the chapter ends inside the mind of the confused and frightened Ikemefuna?

Chapter 3 (pp.16–24)

Summary: *Okonkwo's first venture as a farmer is recounted, as is the death of his father, Unoka.*

The narrative goes back a number of years to Okonkwo's 'start in life' (p.16). Lacking the advantages of other boys whose more industrious fathers could give them barns and seed yams to begin their own farming careers, Okonkwo had to find another way to make his start.

Achebe relates a story about Unoka consulting the Oracle of the Hills and Caves about why his own harvest was always so miserable. Achebe uses anecdotes such as this to reveal important aspects of Ibo culture. It is less important that the priestess tells Unoka that the gods are not angry with him – and that he should 'go home and work like a man' (p.17) – than that we learn about the Ibo's belief in multiple gods and in their speaking through oracles to declare their wishes. We also learn about *chi*, which translates as 'personal god'. *Chi* is one's individual fate; we might refer to a person with good *chi* as 'lucky'. Unoka has bad *chi*, as evidenced by the sorry events of his death; he succumbs to 'swelling', and as this is seen as an 'abomination' to the earth goddess, he is forbidden proper care or burial and is simply carried away to the Evil Forest (pp.17–18). Okonkwo sees this death as shameful and vows that he shall avoid such a fate.

To make his way in the world, Okonkwo has to borrow seed yams from one of the most powerful men in the tribe. This story gives Achebe the opportunity to elaborate on the kind of complicated ritual surrounding such a request (with its ceremony of the kola nut and the palm wine). Note how formal the language is as Okonkwo makes his request. It is particularly interesting the way he and the wealthy villager Nwakibie use so many proverbs; for example, about the toad running in the daytime (p.20) or Eneke the bird (p.21). The Ibo possess a sophisticated culture with complex rituals, an idea reflected in the first chapter, in which Achebe writes, 'Among the Ibo the art of conversation is regarded very highly, and proverbs are the palm-oil with which words are eaten' (p.7).

The remainder of the chapter relates Okonkwo's disastrous first crop in a year that 'had gone mad' (p.23). Unoka's kind words about Okonkwo's perseverance in this crisis are met with contempt.

Q What do we learn about Ibo culture in this chapter?

Chapter 4 (pp.25–34)

Summary: *Ikemefuna settles into his new home; Okonkwo commits a sacrilege during the Week of Peace.*

The chapter begins with a minor incident in which Okonkwo insults a man without titles at a 'kindred meeting' by insinuating that he was *agbala*, an aspersion that reflects Okonkwo's ability 'to kill a man's spirit' (p.25).

After a long illness, Ikemefuna begins to settle into his new home. He is greatly admired by Okonkwo's entire household, including Okonkwo himself. Okonkwo would never show his affection, however, believing that 'to show affection was a sign of weakness' (p.27). Showing his 'strength', he beats his third wife, Ojiugo, for not coming home in time to make the afternoon meal. While this kind of violence is perfectly acceptable to the clan under normal circumstances, what is unacceptable is that Okonkwo has broken the prohibitions of the Week of Peace. The Ibo forefathers have determined that this Week of Peace must be observed before the planting season to ensure a good crop. Admonished by the priest of Ani, the earth goddess, Okonkwo must make sacrifices. It is interesting that though 'inwardly' (p.29) Okonkwo feels repentance for his crime (not for beating his wife, but for doing it when he was not allowed), he does not show it. Okonkwo is so concerned about his image that he is willing to bring upon himself the condemnation of the entire village rather than appear weak.

We gain some knowledge in this chapter of the demands of yam farming and of the planting season. Ikemefuna enthrals everyone in Okonkwo's compound with his many folktales. For the first time, at the end of the chapter, we enter Nwoye's thoughts. He has become very close to Ikemefuna, who sparks his imagination.

Q What does it say about Okonkwo that all the other men take the side of the man he insulted?

Chapter 5 (pp.35–43)

Summary: *The Feast of the New Yam is eagerly awaited; Okonkwo commits an act of violence against his second wife, Ekwefi.*

The clan prepares for the great celebration of the Feast of the New Yam. This is a time to celebrate the new crop by gathering family around and having a feast. Okonkwo is not particularly comfortable at feast occasions. Feeling tense and idle, he finds an excuse to beat his second wife, Ekwefi. When she makes a derogatory comment, he shoots at her with his old hunting gun. Fortunately, the shot lacks accuracy and Ekwefi is not injured by it.

Key point

This incident shows just how violent Okonkwo really is. He beats his wife for no other reason than because he is feeling out of sorts. Contemptible as this is, it is not as frightening as the shooting, which demonstrates that Okonkwo really has no control over his temper. Consider the family completely at the will of this unpredictable and violent man. While much is made in the previous chapter of Okonkwo's breaking the rules of the Week of Peace, nothing is said about how this outburst insults the intentions of the Feast of the New Yam – a time dedicated to giving thanks for family. Achebe leaves us to draw that conclusion ourselves.

Through this incident Achebe looks more closely at Ekwefi and her daughter Ezinma, as he describes domestic life in Okonkwo's compound. Each of Okonkwo's wives raises her own family individually, though the children share general duties with their half-sisters and half-brothers and their mothers.

Q How do roles for women and men differ in Ibo culture?

Q Is Okonkwo's violence depicted as normal behaviour for Ibo men?

Chapter 6 (pp.44–8)

Summary: *The annual wrestling match takes place.*

Wrestling is considered a great, masculine sport, and the annual wrestling matches during the Feast of the New Yam are the highlight of the year. Everyone gathers at the *ilo* (the communal area) to watch the matches, which are accompanied by the beating of many drums. Achebe describes the drummers as being 'possessed by the spirit of the drums' (p.44). His descriptions precisely capture the feeling of intoxication accompanying this scene.

Running in counterpoint to this idea of intoxication is our introduction to Chielo, a woman of the village and friend of Ekwefi who enquires after Ezinma. Perfectly 'normal' now, Chielo also happens to be the 'priestess of Agbala, the Oracle of the Hills and the Caves' (p.46). A little later we will see her become a completely different person under the possession of the oracle. She will play a very important role in the life of Okonkwo's family.

Key point

Achebe is subtly creating a duality between the spiritual and the mundane: there are ordinary objects like drums and there is the otherworldly spirit that possesses their players; there is the 'ancient silk-cotton tree' (p.44) made sacred by the spirit of good children waiting to be born; and there is an otherwise normal woman, Chielo, who happens to be inhabited by the spirit of Agbala. Achebe wants us to see through the mundane appearance of things to the spiritual identity contained within.

Q In what ways is music important to the Ibo?

Chapter 7 (pp.49–58)

Summary: *Word comes from the Oracle of the Hills and Caves that the boy Ikemefuna must be killed.*

After three years with Okonkwo's family, Ikemefuna has become one of them. Okonkwo has noted the positive effect Ikemefuna has had on Nwoye, who he wants 'to grow into a tough young man capable of ruling his father's household' (p.49). We follow Achebe into Nwoye's thoughts to discover a little more about the kinds of folk stories he loved to hear from his mother when he was a young child. Though he is being compelled to give up such things, Nwoye does not feel ready yet to embrace the masculine, violent life for which he is being raised. A distinct contrast is drawn between his mother's stories and the bloody tales Okonkwo tells him and Ikemefuna after dinner in his *obi* (the large hut in which the head of the family lives).

In the midst of a very rare occurrence, the coming of great swarms of locusts (welcomed by the people of Umuofia, as locusts are a great delicacy), Okonkwo receives word from Ezeudu, the oldest man in Umuofia, that the Oracle of the Hills and Caves has pronounced that Ikemefuna must be killed. This old man advises Okonkwo to take no part in the killing itself because 'that boy calls you father' (p.54).

The next day, Ikemefuna is led away from the villages of Umuofia, having been told that he will be returned to Mbaino. Achebe brings us into Ikemefuna's mind; this poignant scene echoes the one three years earlier when he was separated from his family and taken to Umuofia. Having come to think of Okonkwo's compound as his home, Ikemefuna does not know what to expect any more in Mbaino. He plays a little game, so reminiscent of childhood, stepping out the rhythm of a song to try to determine if his mother is still alive. Okonkwo has not heeded Ezeudu's advice; he is present, but looks away when the first blow falls. Understandably, Ikemefuna runs to the man he calls 'father' for protection. It is then that Okonkwo delivers the fatal strike with his matchet, 'afraid of being thought weak' (p.57).

The immediate aftermath of the killing is seen through the point of view of Nwoye, who realises as soon as his father comes home what has happened: 'something seemed to give way inside [Nwoye], like the snapping of a tightened bow. He did not cry. He just hung limp' (p.58). His devastation takes the form of a great emptiness. The only other time he experienced such emptiness was when he once heard the cry of a baby in the Evil Forest, one of a set of twins that the Ibo religion condemned as evil and dictated must be abandoned there in earthenware jars.

Q Why do you think the Ibo accept the decree from the Oracle of the Hills and Caves without question?

Q In what ways is Ikemefuna's fate symbolic of the fate of the Ibo?

Chapter 8 (pp.59–70)

Summary: *Life continues as normal in the village after the murder of Ikemefuna.*

Okonkwo is greatly affected by the killing of Ikemefuna – at least for a few days. Soon enough he is back to normal and berating himself for the self-indulgence of grief:

> 'When did you become a shivering old woman,' Okonkwo asked himself, 'you are known in all the nine villages for your valour in war. How can a man who has killed five men in battle fall to pieces because he has added a boy to their number? Okonkwo, you have become a woman indeed.' (pp.60–1)

This self-criticism gives us a glimpse into how Okonkwo makes himself such a hard man. He seeks company from his friend Obierika and faults him for not taking part in the killing of Ikemefuna. Obierika responds with an accusation of his own:

> If I were you I would have stayed at home. What you have done will not please the Earth. It is the kind of action for which the goddess wipes out whole families. (pp.62–3)

The rest of the chapter is devoted to another complex ritual: the bargaining for a bride by her parents and a young man's parents. Marriages are arranged in Umuofia, and there are many formalities to be gone through. Achebe looks at the subject through the differing perspectives of the man's realm (they haggle in the *obi* over palm wine) and the women's realm (as the intended bride proves her worth as a cook).

Q Is Obierika right in his criticism of Okonkwo's actions?

Q What part does the killing of Ikemefuna play in the fortunes of Okonkwo?

Chapter 9 (pp.71–82)

Summary: *Ezinma, Okonkwo's daughter, almost dies; the story of Ekwefi's struggle to conceive is recounted.*

A few days after the killing, Okonkwo is woken in the morning to the news that Ezinma is dying. This does not turn out to be the case; the girl has *iba* (fever). We are told the sad and fascinating story of Ekwefi's children: nine have died in infancy, with Ezinma, who is now about ten, the only one to have lived beyond three years. The names Ekwefi gives to these children – such as Onwumbiko: 'Death, I implore you' (p.73) – attest to the increasing force of her despair.

A medicine man consulted after the death of the second child determines that Ekwefi has been giving birth repeatedly to the *same* child, to an *ogbanje* (changeling), 'one of those wicked children who, when they died, entered their mothers' wombs to be born again' (p.73). He tries to break the cycle using a number of different remedies, to no avail, until Ezinma is born. She carries one of the telling characteristics of an *ogbanje*, in that she is sickly.

This episode offers a fascinating lesson on how different cultures explain the same phenomenon. In an isolated, agrarian society such as that of the Ibo, the infant mortality rate would be enormously high compared to our own in the modern West. Dying infants would not be uncommon. But when a woman loses many children, some explanation must be found. In the modern West we would look to the mother's health as the cause. The Ibo look to the spirit world.

Achebe never makes judgements in his novel about the efficacy of Ibo beliefs. He depicts these beliefs, such as the Ibo explanation for Ekwefi's plight and the story of *iyi-uwa* (an object that binds an *ogbanje* to the human world, causing it to be reborn to the same mother), as complex and consistent.

Q What does Okonkwo's relationship with Ezinma reveal about his character?

Chapter 10 (pp.83–9)

Summary: *The* egwugwu*, or ancestral spirits of the village, perform a judgement in a civil case.*

Achebe shows us the way the Ibo settle particularly difficult civil cases. Nine of the most prominent men (representing the nine villages of the clan) masquerade as spirits. Their masks and costumes are kept in a special hut to which women are denied entry; it is the home of the 'most secret cult in the clan' (p.84). While these spirits are familiar men in costume, it seems that on a religious level, the Ibo accept these figures unreservedly as spirits. The sight of them all together at the one time makes the women instinctively take 'to their heels' (p.84).

The appearance of these men is not just ceremonial. Achebe shows us how the *egwugwu* settle a difficult domestic dispute that could not be solved otherwise. This ritual may seem odd at first, but it certainly has civil merit. After all, the case is being tried by nine of the leading citizens – one would be hard-pressed to come up with a better method for adjudicating a case in a clan where everyone knows everyone else. Likewise, it has parallels with our own system: judges and barristers in Australia wear robes and wigs to distinguish them as officers of the court and to identify them with the institutions of the state.

Q What role do the *egwugwu* play in everyday life?

Chapter 11 (pp.90–103)

Summary: *Chielo, as the priestess of Agbala, the Oracle of the Hills and Caves, takes Ezinma for a mysterious ritual.*

In this chapter, Achebe returns us from the civil sphere into the domestic sphere. Ekwefi tells a folktale of Tortoise and the birds to Ezinma, who has recovered from her fever. In allocating so much of the chapter to this story, Achebe gives us another glimpse into the mythology of the Ibo, but also further explores an important theme of the novel. Remember that the story Ekwefi is telling her daughter is the kind of tale that Okonkwo insists Nwoye must leave behind if he is to become a man. This is one of the central conflicts in Nwoye's life, and Okonkwo's rigid demarcation of the woman's world and the man's world (these stories obviously belong with the former) contribute to the son's increasing isolation and alienation from his father.

When it is Ezinma's turn to tell a story, a wailing is heard out in the dark night; it is Chielo, in the throes of possession by Agbala, coming to take Ezinma. Where Chielo's 'power' has been alluded to in previous chapters, now we see it in full force. Remember, it is through this woman that the order to kill Ikemefuna was given. Now she has come for Ezinma, and if we were not yet convinced of the depth of Ekwefi's bond to her only child, we must be now. Overcoming her deep fear of the dark night, she follows the ghostly form of Chielo with Ezinma on her back on an aimless path leading eventually to the shrine. However, not even her deep concern as a mother can overcome her terror or her respect for Agbala's domain, and these deeply held beliefs prevent her from entering the cave.

Achebe shows us again the complex duality in the lives of the Ibo. Beneath the surface of the 'everyday' is a mysterious and powerful spirit world. Contact between these two worlds is frequent and immediate, and it can be devastating. Nothing better exemplifies this duality than Ekwefi's thoughts about Chielo:

> Chielo's voice rose again in her possessed chanting, and Ekwefi recoiled, because there was no humanity there. It was not the same Chielo who sat with her in the market and sometimes bought bean-cakes for Ezinma, whom she called her daughter. It was a different woman – the priestess of Agbala, the Oracle of the Hills and Caves. (p.101)

The chapter ends with Ekwefi's realisation that her husband Okonkwo has also traced the steps of Chielo. He has been as worried as she has about their daughter (as explained in the next chapter). The bond between them here serves as a striking contrast to the episode in Chapter 5 when Okonkwo beats Ekwefi and then attempts to shoot her.

Q What does this chapter tell us about the importance of religious beliefs in Ibo culture?

Chapter 12 (pp.104–12)

Summary: *The wedding of Obierika's daughter takes place.*

Most of the wedding preparations are undertaken by the women of the village. We see again the extent to which Ibo duties are defined as belonging to men or women. While everyone is invited, Achebe tells us that it is 'really a woman's ceremony and the central figures were the bride and her mother' (p.104). We hear the story of the strong medicine of the village of Umuike that makes their market the most popular among the villages. We also see another example of Ibo law when the cry goes out that a cow has broken loose. This is a more serious problem than it might at first seem. Remember that the Ibo depend on their yam crop to live. A cow loose in the fields can cause a lot of damage. Leaving five of their group behind to watch the cooking pots, the rest of the women go out to return the cow to its owner, from whom they exact 'the heavy fine which the village imposed on anyone whose cow was let loose on his neighbours' crops' (p.108). It is certainly interesting that the Ibo have legislated what the fine for such an offence will be; perhaps more interesting, though, is the way that all the women of the village must be accounted for. It also seems to be the rule that when the cry of *'Oji odu achu iiiji-o-o!'* (p.108) goes up, every woman in the town must respond to it.

The wedding itself is characterised by ritual and celebration: the palm wine ceremony between Obierika and the men of the groom's family; the singing of the praises of the elders of the village (Okonkwo included); and the dance of the girls and, eventually, the bride – all to the accompaniment of music.

Q Are women's roles in Ibo culture severely limited in comparison to men's roles?

Chapter 13 (pp.113–18)

Summary: *Okonkwo accidentally kills one of the mourners at Ezeudu's funeral.*

On the heels of the joyous scenes of the wedding comes the announcement that one of the great men of the tribe, Ezeudu, has died. The funeral of this warrior is marked by hysteria, particularly in the men. Indeed, where other Ibo ceremonies are notable in adhering so closely to a defined program, this funeral seems to be utterly chaotic:

> The ancient drums of death beat, guns and cannon were fired, and men dashed about in frenzy, cutting down every tree or animal they saw, jumping over walls and dancing on the roof. (p.114)

The *egwugwu* appear as well, signifying that the death of a great warrior is a cause for mourning even by the gods. Again, we see how close their world is to that of the Ibo:

> The land of the living was not far removed from the domain of the ancestors. There was coming and going between them, especially at festivals and also when an old man died, because an old man was very close to the ancestors. (p.115)

The speech from the most frightening of the *egwugwu*, addressed to the dead Ezeudu, indicates that the Ibo believe in reincarnation (p.116).

Note how one of the *egwugwu* must be restrained by two men from inflicting serious harm with his matchet. The overall feeling of this ceremony is that *almost* anything goes, as long as no-one is seriously hurt. But then the unthinkable occurs. While all the men are firing their guns, Okonkwo's explodes and a piece of iron kills one of Ezeudu's sons dancing farewell to his father. In one moment, the life of his family is changed; though the killing is accidental, Okonkwo must flee the clan in shame. The earth decrees that Okonkwo's compound must be destroyed by men of the village dressed for war.

In the space of a few hours, everything has indeed 'fallen apart' for Okonkwo. There is some irony in that, though he is known for his skills as a warrior, Okonkwo is also known to be useless with a gun.

Key point

There is more irony in the fact that, not long before this accident, Okonkwo had tried to shoot Ekwefi with this same gun. It is almost as if fate is paying him back for that indiscretion. One should also bear in mind the heated words of Obierika after Okonkwo's killing of Ikemefuna: 'It is the kind of action for which the goddess wipes out whole families' (p.63).

Q Is Okonkwo's banishment an act of revenge by the goddess for the killing of Ikemefuna?

PART TWO

Chapter 14 (pp.121–7)

Summary: *Okonkwo's family moves to their new home in Mbanta.*

There is something fitting in Okonkwo's decision to seek protection in Mbanta, the village of his mother. We have seen the close relationships between mothers and their children in his own compound, but Okonkwo, so obsessed with manliness, dismisses anything having to do with women.

This period of banishment might be read as one of enforced recognition of the female realm. Uchendu, Okonkwo's mother's brother – the head of the Mbanto branch of the family – makes a powerful welcoming speech in which he reflects on the importance of mothers:

> A man belongs to his fatherland when things are good and life is sweet. But when there is sorrow and bitterness he finds refuge in his motherland ... And that is why we say that mother is supreme. (p.126)

Uchendu concludes his speech with the lines of a song sung when a woman dies:

> *For whom is it well, for whom is it well?*
> *There is no one for whom it is well.* (p.127)

Though its sentiments are slightly different, these lines are reminiscent of John Donne's famous words (from *Devotions upon Emergent Occasions*), also intoned at funerals: 'No man is an island, entire of itself ... and therefore never send to know for whom the bell tolls; it tolls for thee.'

Q What does this chapter tell us about the role of mothers in Ibo culture?

Chapter 15 (pp.128–34)

Summary: *Obierika comes to visit Okonkwo and tells the story of the destruction of the village of Abame by white men.*

The pace of the narrative increases dramatically in Part Two. The events in this chapter occur a year or so after those in Chapter 14. Obierika, who has been looking after Okonkwo's farm back in Umuofia, comes to visit with cowries (money) from his sharecroppers. In the course of their discussions, Obierika relates the destruction of the village of Abame by white men. This story obviously carries a glimpse into the future. The Ibo have heard of the white men, primarily in stories related to the slave trade. But they have no firsthand knowledge of Europeans, as the land of the Ibo, in Eastern Nigeria, is away from the slave-gathering regions. It seems that Europeans have now come into the region with other intentions.

The reactions of Uchendu and Okonkwo to Obierika's story are interesting in their difference. Uchendu calls the men of Abame 'fools' (p.131) because they killed a man (a European intruder) who did not say anything. He then relates a folktale about Mother Kite and her daughter to prove his point. Okonkwo considers the men of Achebe foolish for having been caught unarmed even after being warned by the oracle 'that danger was ahead' (p.132). Here Uchendu represents the perception of the world through folk tradition (the 'female' Ibo principle), while Okonkwo sees things through a warrior's eyes (the 'male' Ibo principle).

The chapter closes with another unsettling exchange. Okonkwo does not know how to thank his friend for looking after his affairs, to which Obierika jokingly responds: 'Kill one of your sons for me' (p.133). When Okonkwo suggests 'that will not be enough', Obierika makes his final joke: 'then kill yourself' (p.134). Beneath the banter lurk the twin ghosts of the past and the future, of Ikemefuna's death and Okonkwo's eventual fate.

Q In what ways are Uchendu and Okonkwo different?

Chapter 16 (pp.135–9)

Summary: *The Europeans firmly establish themselves in Mbanto as missionaries; Nwoye is converted to the new religion.*

Narrative time is compressed even further, with this chapter taking place two years after the last one. In that time, British missionaries have established themselves among the Ibo in Umuofia; they have built a church and converted a 'handful' (p.135) of people. At first it is only the *efulefu*, those whom the tribe define as 'worthless, empty men' (p.135), who join the Christians. Obierika is surprised to see Nwoye among them one day. This prompts a visit to Mbanto, but Okonkwo will not speak about his son. Achebe then ventures back in time to tell us the story of how Nwoye came to Christianity.

Marked by dialogue and hymn singing, the first interaction between the white missionary and the Ibo is quite comical, with the missionary saying 'my buttocks' in Ibo when he means to say 'myself' (p.136). His listeners question him in a generally lighthearted way; most of them seem to come away with the same impression Okonkwo forms that afternoon, that the missionaries are mad. Note how Achebe writes about this first contact from the Ibo perspective, conveying the sense of utter strangeness of the religious principles the Christian espouses. (It is the concept of the Trinity – over which even many of the most devout believers have been scratching their heads for more than a millennium – that most convinces the Ibo that the man is crazy.)

The primitive aggression in the missionary's approach to the Ibo's complex religion – 'Your gods are not alive and cannot do you any harm ... They are pieces of wood and stone' (p.138) – paints him as a conqueror. However, something other than the missionary's attack wins over Nwoye:

> It was not the mad logic of the Trinity that captivated him. He did not understand it. It was the poetry of the new religion, something felt in the marrow. The hymn about brothers who sat in darkness and in fear seemed to answer a vague and persistent question that haunted his young soul – the question of the twins crying in the bush and the question of Ikemefuna who was killed. He felt a relief within as the hymn poured into his parched soul. (p.139)

Q How has the arrival of British missionaries changed life in Umuofia?

Chapter 17 (pp.140–5)

Summary: *The missionaries are given a portion of the Evil Forest to build a church; Okonkwo reacts to Nwoye's conversion.*

When the white missionary and his convert ask the elders of Mbanta for a piece of land on which to build their church, Uchendu gets the idea to offer them as much of the Evil Forest as they care to take, because 'nobody in his right senses' (p.140) would ever accept such an offer. To the clan's surprise, the Christians are not struck dead, not even after seven market weeks (the traditional time past which no spirit would wait to exact revenge). The Christians begin to win converts, including their first woman, named Nneka. She is pregnant, and she has already borne four sets of twins left to die in the forest.

After Nwoye is seen with the Christians, Okonkwo begins to beat him severely. Surprisingly, the stern voice of Uchendu makes him stop. Nothing to this point has made Okonkwo stop a beating once he has begun it, not even the offended spirits of the Week of Peace. That he is restrained by Uchendu indicates the extent to which Okonkwo feels cowed in the land of his mother.

Given the chance to think over the matter of his son's conversion in peace, Okonkwo comes to an interesting conclusion:

> He, Okonkwo, was called a flaming fire. How could he have begotten a woman for a son? ... And immediately Okonkwo's eyes were opened and he saw the whole matter clearly. Living fire begets cold, impotent ash. (p.145)

Q What is the significance of Nwoye leaving his culture behind and converting to Christianity?

Chapter 18 (pp.146–52)

Summary: *The first act of violence erupts between the clan and the converts; a white civil authority is set up in Umuofia.*

As the church grows in Mbanta, tensions heighten between them and the clan, though the latter is still willing to let the Christians practise their religion in peace. It is when some of the zealous converts begin to threaten to destroy the Ibo shrines that they are badly beaten. However, converts are still considered to be members of the clan. There can be no question of their being killed. We learn about an entire class of people called *osu*, outcasts of the clan. Curiously, some of the new converts carry their revulsion of the *osu* with them into the new religion, insisting that the outcasts should not be admitted. Mr Kiaga, who is in charge of the Mbanta church, holds firm in his belief that 'we are all children of God and we must receive these our brothers' (p.147), and soon all the *osu* convert to Christianity.

One of these recent converts is accused of killing the 'royal python' (p.149) – there is some irony in the fact that this sacred animal is addressed by the Ibo as 'Our Father'. This creates a crisis for the elders of Mbanto; no agreed punishment exists for such an act because 'nobody thought that such a thing could ever happen' (p.149). It is decided that the Christians should be ostracised. This looks like it will lead to increased violence, but the man accused of killing the python falls ill and dies. The clan is satisfied that 'the gods were still able to fight their own battles' (p.152).

Q How does this chapter show the Ibo belief in gods influencing everyday life?

Q Why do some of the converted tribe members continue to shun the *osu*?

Chapter 19 (pp.153–8)

Summary: *Okonkwo's seven years of exile come to an end; he and his family prepare for their return to Umuofia.*

Okonkwo's last act in Mbanta will be to have a great feast to thank his mother's kinsmen for taking in the family in their time of hardship. The words of a nameless elder, one of Uchendu's generation, on this occasion are well chosen:

> A man who calls his kinsmen to a feast does not do so to save them from starving. They all have food in their own homes ... We come together because it is good for kinsmen to do so ... But I fear for you young people because you do not understand how strong is the bond of kinship. You do not know what it is to speak with one voice. (p.157)

Key point

In the seven years since Okonkwo came to Mbanto, the elders have witnessed unprecedented and entirely unpredictable events that now threaten the tribe's unity. The new religion is dividing them. Things are falling apart.

Q Is the importance of kinship already lost on the young people of the tribe, even before colonisation has occurred?

PART THREE

Chapter 20 (pp.161–7)

Summary: *Okonkwo and his family return to Umuofia to find sweeping change; the British have established the village as the centre of their new government.*

Though his ambitions to become one of Umuofia's greatest men suffered a serious setback during his period of exile, Okonkwo believes that he will be able to regain his stature upon return. However, when he returns to Umuofia, he finds that the social landscape has undergone considerable change. He learns that the church there has made inroads, and that now even men of high standing are converting. The story of one such man, Ogbuefi Ugonna, is humorous: believing that the sacrament of Holy Communion would be an Ibo-style 'feast', he had brought his drinking-horn along with him (p.164). It underscores that even after seven years, the relationship between the Ibo and the missionaries is still often based on comical misunderstanding.

Not humorous, however, is the kind of interaction occurring between the provisional government of the District Commissioner and the Ibo. More and more of the Ibo are being imprisoned for things they do not recognise as crimes (including the leaving of twins in the Evil Forest). The District Commissioner judges their cases in what the Ibo perceive to be ignorance; they are treated harshly and subject to humiliation, particularly by *kotma*, those who act as 'court messengers' (p.164). These non-Ibo Nigerians from other parts of the colony are the most hated of all.

When Obierika informs Okonkwo of all these developments, Okonkwo judges his clan by his own inclinations and wonders why they have lost the will to fight and drive out the white men. However, his friend sees that the situation is much more complicated:

> Our own men and our sons have joined the ranks of the stranger ... If we should try to drive out the white men in Umuofia we should find it easy. There are only two of them. But what of our own people who are following their way and have been given power? (p.165)

They discuss the case of a man who was hanged by the District Commissioner after he murdered someone over a land dispute. The implication is that the man, Aneto, lost his case because the other side had bribed the court messengers, and then he revenged himself on a member of the other party, Oduche. Contrast this case with the one that occurs in Chapter 10. In that dispute, the *egwugwu* adjudicated the case in a way that was acceptable to all parties.

Key point

Achebe is not explicitly stating that one justice system is better than the other, but note that when the *egwugwu* judge a case, no-one feels they have been cheated; this time, Aneto's violent action results from his feeling of being deprived of justice by a corrupt and ignorant civil authority.

The changes that Okonkwo sees around him are directly attributable to the arrival of the European settlers, who regard Ibo customs as 'bad' (p.166). Obierika suggests that infiltration was facilitated by the shrewdness of the Europeans and the naivety of the Ibo in allowing them to stay:

> The white man is very clever. He came quietly and peaceably with his religion. We were amused at his foolishness and allowed him to stay. Now he has won our brothers, and our clan can no longer act like one. He has put a knife on the things that held us together and we have fallen apart. (p.166)

Q What does Chapter 20 tell us about the ability of colonisers to change the culture of the colonised?

Chapter 21 (pp.168–73)

Summary: *The state of affairs in Umuofia is further explored; an interesting discussion about religion is conducted by the missionary, Mr Brown, and respected Ibo man Akunna; Okonkwo's homecoming is not what he expected.*

Obierika noted in his last speech that the white men had softened the Ibo with religion, thus leaving them vulnerable to the rest of their designs. Here we see a little more of that process. Along with the European colonisers comes the opportunity to make money: 'for the first time palm-oil and kernel became things of great price, and much money flowed into Umuofia' (p.168).

Key point

Achebe shows how the coloniser gains complete control of the colonised culture. It cannot be done with the sword alone, though of course any coloniser understands the necessity of force. This aspect of colonisation is far more insidious and lasting. It makes the colonised people totally dependent on the new ways of the coloniser; it conquers by changing them – into Christians, into capitalists.

Just as the matter of religious differences is beginning to seem less important, Achebe introduces Mr Brown, the white missionary who has gained respect from the Ibo through his willingness to listen. A discussion he has with Akunna, one of the great men of the nine villages, offers an interesting glimpse into the differences and similarities between the two religions. Akunna attempts to refute the standard missionary attack that the Ibo worship pieces of wood: 'It is indeed a piece of wood. The tree from which it came was made by Chukwu, as indeed all minor gods were. But He made them for His messengers so that we could approach Him through them' (p.169). Akunna contends that all worship of minor deities is merely a way of worshipping the one god, Chukwu: 'It is right to do so. We approach a great man through his servants' (p.170).

Brown's increasing knowledge of the Ibo's spiritual practices enables him to recognise that it will not succumb to a 'frontal attack' (p.170). So he devises a plan that involves another crucial branch in the tree of colonisation – education – by playing on Ibo fears that those who are not educated will be left behind when control shifts completely to the British authorities: 'If Umuofia failed to send her children to the school, strangers would come from other places to rule them' (p.171). The irony is that these words come from a British missionary supported by a brutal civil authority. Regardless, the Ibo of Umuofia send their children (and themselves) to Brown's school, showing that nothing is more powerful than education in the British goal of transforming the culture.

Okonkwo is made despondent by the changes he sees: 'He mourned for the clan, which he saw breaking up and falling apart, and he mourned for the warlike men of Umuofia, who had so unaccountably become soft like women' (p.173).

Q Is Mr Brown sincerely interested in learning about the Ibo religion?

Chapter 22 (pp.174–81)

Summary: *Mr Brown's replacement sees things differently from his predecessor and incites a crisis between church and clan.*

When an ailing Mr Brown is replaced by the hardline zealot Mr Smith (note Achebe's use of the most ordinary English names, denoting the utter facelessness of these 'servants of the Lord'), things change quite dramatically. Achebe writes the first two paragraphs in this chapter using the kind of rhetoric the firebrand Smith engages in: 'He believed in slaying the prophets of Baal' (p.174). Smith is a mindless fountain of doctrine who allows zealous converts such as Enoch (who had been restrained under Brown's tenure) to cause havoc.

Enoch unmasks one of the *egwugwu* during a tribal ritual. This is a great sin for the Ibo, amounting to the death of the ancestral spirit (a fact Enoch would have known):

> That night the Mother of the Spirits walked the length and breadth of the clan, weeping for her murdered son ... It seemed as if the very soul of the tribe wept for a great evil that was coming – its own death. (pp.176–7)

The following day, the *egwugwu* destroy Enoch's compound and head for the church. Achebe lets us into the thoughts of Smith in his moment of great fear and doubt. He very nearly flees, but in the end stands his ground. The *egwugwu* do not harm him, but they burn down the church.

Q How does the statement, 'You can stay with us if you like our ways. You can worship your own god. It is good that a man should worship the gods and the spirits of his fathers' (p.180) made by Ajofia, the chief of the *egwugwu*, compare with Mr Smith's philosophy of 'black and white' (p.174)?

Chapter 23 (pp.182–7)

Summary: *The men of the tribe who burned down the church are arrested and detained.*

Okonkwo is made 'almost happy' (p.182) by the actions of the *egwugwu*. While they did not kill the Christians as he had counselled, they took action. Not many days later, the District Commissioner asks the leaders of the tribe to his headquarters for what he calls a 'palaver' (p.183), only to have the six men arrested. He passes judgement on their actions and imprisons them until they agree to surrender the fine he levies against them.

While the Commissioner's tactics are contemptible, the arbitrary nature with which he dispenses 'justice' is much more alarming. Explaining to them that the British have brought to the Ibo 'a court of law where we judge cases and administer justice just as it is done in my own country under a great queen' (p.184), he hands down his verdict to men who have not had the benefit of counsel or fair hearing (in other words, in a fashion vastly different from that practised in the English judicial system). The message is quite clear: the District Commissioner's court is one of English law in name only. He then leaves the men of Umuofia to the mercy of his merciless court messengers. These men take it upon themselves to 'shake down' the village for an extra fifty bags of cowries by threatening the execution of the held men – a threat that not even the District Commissioner had made.

Q In what ways do Ibo law and British law differ?

Chapter 24 (pp.188–94)

Summary: *The prisoners return, furious; a village council is called to determine the kind of response Umuofia will make to their arrest and imprisonment; Okonkwo kills a court messenger sent to break up the meeting.*

This chapter provides insight into both the power and the futility of words and speech. Okonkwo burns with hatred and a desire for revenge on the Commissioner and his messengers. He takes out his war dress and remembers the great words spoken in the past by Okudo, who 'sang a war song in a way that no other man could ... his voice turned every man into a lion' (p.189). In contrast to this is Egonwanne, whom Okonkwo assumes will speak the following day when the men of Umuofia will meet to decide on their response to the District Commissioner's actions: 'His sweet tongue can change fire into cold ash. When he speaks he moves our men to impotence' (p.190). Okonkwo is not a man of words but of action (remember, he stammers when he gets too excited). In Okonkwo's view, words are for women, and discussions and counsel with the white men are what has gotten Umuofia into this deplorable situation.

The next day at the meeting Okonkwo hardly speaks to his friends, Obierika included. The speeches are just underway (the first is by a man called Okika who incites the men of Umuofia to declare war on the British) when five court messengers come to break up the meeting under orders from the District Commissioner. Okonkwo, at the edge of the crowd, meets them 'trembling with hate, unable to utter a word' (p.194). In two strokes of his matchet, he beheads the lead messenger.

Amid the speeches of the council, Okonkwo acts without a single word. And it is the words that follow that tell him the old Umuofia is gone forever:

> Okonkwo stood looking at the dead man. He knew that Umuofia would not go to war. He knew because they had let the other messengers escape. They had broken into tumult instead of action … He heard voices asking: 'Why did he do it?' (p.194)

Q What does this chapter tell us about the importance of words?

Q Why does Okonkwo feel that the Ibo culture is lost?

Q Do you sympathise with Okonkwo? Why or why not?

Chapter 25 (pp.195–7)

Summary: *When the District Commissioner comes with his men to arrest Okonkwo, they find that he has hanged himself.*

This short chapter gives us the sad final scene in the protagonist's life. It should not be assumed that Okonkwo hangs himself out of fear of arrest or due to regret for the crime he has committed. Rather, he kills himself in despair for the lost ways of his clan. He has watched them turn from a proud people to a subjugated people.

Key point

One of the more insidious ways that colonisers maintain control over the colonised is by forcing them into situations where their only option is to act unnaturally. Eventually doubt and confusion take root until the indigenous people may really believe themselves backwards and inferior. They become strangers in their own country, the servants of a dominant culture that has changed everything. Though he never expresses this, it is this realisation of the plight of his people, made clear through Achebe's narration, that directly causes Okonkwo to take his own life.

Achebe hints at the consuming influence of colonial culture by writing the final paragraph as though through the consciousness of the District Commissioner, which reinforces the idea that this world does not belong to the Ibo any longer – it belongs to the British. The paragraph is loaded with irony, as we follow the thoughts of a man who is working on a book to be titled *The Pacification of the Primitive Tribes of the Lower Niger*. Contrast his imaginary book – the one that will not devote even a chapter to the 'man who had killed a messenger and hanged himself' (p.197) – to this one by Achebe, a book that looks deeply into the ways of the Ibo, without judgement. The book to be written by the Commissioner can be thought of as a metaphor for the colonial paradigm. Like the British, or any colonisers, this man will take what he wants from the 'primitive' culture and turn it into the story of the 'white man's burden', of the enlightenment and correction of a savage people.

And what of Okonkwo? Think of the irony implicit in his death. His own tribesmen will not touch his body for fear of spiritual contamination. Strangers will bury the remains, and sacrifices to cleanse the earth will have to be made. One recalls the fate of the man for whom Okonkwo felt such shame and loathing, his father Unoka, left to rot in the Evil Forest.

Q In what ways will the District Commissioner's recounting of African culture differ from the one provided by Achebe?

CHARACTERS & RELATIONSHIPS

Okonkwo

Key quotes

'Perhaps down in his heart Okonkwo was not a cruel man. But his whole life was dominated by fear, the fear of failure and of weakness.' (pp.12–13)

'His life had been ruled by a great passion – to become one of the lords of the clan ... Then everything had been broken ... Here was a man whose *chi* said nay despite his own affirmation.' (p.123)

'He mourned for the clan, which he saw breaking up and falling apart, and he mourned for the warlike men of Umuofia, who had so unaccountably become soft like women.' (p.173)

Okonkwo, the protagonist of *Things Fall Apart*, is a hard man. He is brutal and unforgiving, even with members of his own family. He is also supremely ambitious; he wants to become the leader in his tribe, take the most titles, grow the most yams and produce the most sons. The source of his ambition is an almost debilitating fear of failure. Seemingly contradictory to this fear of failure is Okonkwo's inability to doubt even for a moment that he is right – about anything, from the way he runs his family, terrorising his wives and children, to his decision to take part in the killing of Ikemefuna. This inflexibility is perhaps his most persistent character trait – the factor that leads more than anything else to his tragic end.

The fear of failure that drives Okonkwo is really a fear of appearing to be what he thinks of as 'womanish'. Okonkwo, somewhat ironically, resembles Mr Smith in the way he sees things only in 'black and white' (p.174) – that is, without any grey, or middle ground. To be manly is to be strong and self-reliant, to rule one's house with terror, to never listen to a word of objection from a woman or child and to be ambitious. The 'womanish' would denote just about everything else. This simplistic position stems from Okonkwo's fear of appearing similar to his father, Unoka. Okonkwo cannot see past Unoka's negative characteristics (his laziness, improvidence and cowardliness) to accept any of his positive characteristics (his kindness and his love of company, conversation, beauty and music). In Okonkwo's eyes, anything associated with Unoka is 'womanish' and contemptible.

It is important to note that Okonkwo is an unbalanced character. Given his success and high standing in the tribe, it is tempting to think of him as representative of the Ibo people as a whole; however, his inflexibility makes him something of an outsider. He cannot appreciate or truly take part in certain crucial aspects of the Ibo culture, namely their generous conversation and sense of kinship, and their appreciation of the world through the lens of their rich folk tradition. Okonkwo's separation from the driving spirit of the Umuofia tribe is most evident in the following events, occurring before the incursion of the white men into their territory:

- the violation of the Week of Peace, when he beats his wife Ojiugo (Chapter 4)
- the attempt to shoot Ekwefi in a fit of anger (Chapter 5)
- his participation in the killing of Ikemefuna (because he did not want to appear weak) despite being advised against doing so (Chapter 7).

Okonkwo as tragic hero

There is some value in comparing Okonkwo to figures of Greek tragedy such as Oedipus, Medea or Agamemnon. Achebe's portrayal seems to encourage such a comparison. Greek tragic heroes are usually in positions of power. They are also notable for possessing what has been called the 'tragic flaw', a negative character trait (e.g. pride, ambition or anger) that leads to their ultimate fall. In Okonkwo's case, violence and inflexibility are his tragic flaws. Tragic heroes are also subject to fate – to things that seem predetermined by the gods. Often the gods of Greek tragedies seem to play mercilessly with the fate of tragic heroes. However, it is usually because these characters attempt to step out of or beyond the roles they are assigned (as tragic flaws take these characters outside the mould of 'normal' and acceptable human behaviour) that they draw the retribution of the gods in the first place. Thus a combination of fate and the tragic flaw is what leads to the ruin of a tragic hero. This is reflected in Obierika's words after Okonkwo takes part in the killing of Ikemefuna: 'It is the kind of action for which the goddess wipes out whole families' (p.63).

Without question, there is an aura of the tragic hero about Okonkwo – not just in his noticeable tragic flaw (and the fact that it leads to his destruction) or in his challenging the propriety of his gods and his society, but also in the way that he is completely subject to fate. This latter element is illustrated in the event that precipitates Okonkwo's exile: the accidental killing of the son of Ezeudu during the latter's funeral. Often, in classic tragedy, this is just the way the gods work; they pick a punishment that is within the province of 'bad luck', yet is somehow fitting. The same gun with which Okonkwo *tried* to kill Ekwefi is the one that inadvertently kills Ezeudu's son.

This aura of classic tragedy is one reason why readers may find themselves identifying with Okonkwo by the end of the novel. Readers identify with the tragic hero, even as they revile them for their tragic flaw, because their characteristics and stories are portrayed in a magnified or emphasised way in order to highlight a particular aspect of human nature. In their struggle against the gods (one they have no hope of winning), they embody the losing battle we all fight against fate and its crude henchman, death. By the end of *Things Fall Apart*, despite Okonkwo's status as an outsider within the clan, he does indeed come to represent his people in the eyes of the reader. Paradoxically, this occurs because of the very character trait that isolates him – his inflexibility.

Key point

Okonkwo refuses to consider being enticed by offers of education, wealth and stability, with which the colonisers lure so many of the Ibo away. His inflexibility comes to represent the persistence and determination that had once held the Ibo culture so strongly together. By the end, because he is fighting against so contemptible and overwhelming an enemy, Okonkwo's inflexibility takes on a heroic dimension.

Yet in the end, his resistance is, ironically, the thing that separates him again from his people. Think about how carefully Achebe has created this character. In Chapter 24 the messenger comes to break up the meeting of the tribesmen. Okonkwo cuts off his head – it is almost inconceivable that Okonkwo could do anything else. It is really the only thing consistent with his character. But no-one follows his lead – the gesture of violence and inflexibility isolates him from his clan. Again, it is not due to fear of the new authority that Okonkwo hangs himself; it is out of despair for the change that has occurred in his people. Still, this last act, bred from violent passion, is also within character. It fulfils the complex pattern for the downfall of the tragic hero – partly destroyed by fate, partly by tragic flaw.

Unoka

Key quotes

'In his day he was lazy and improvident and was quite incapable of thinking about tomorrow.' (p.4)

'Unoka would play with [the musicians], his face beaming with blessedness and peace.' (p.4)

'He died and rotted away above the earth, and was not given the first or the second burial ... When they carried him away, he took with him his flute.' (p.18)

Okonkwo's father, Unoka, is generally seen through the eyes of the son who hates him. But Achebe gives him a fair hearing in the first chapter of the novel. Unoka did not take any titles during his life. This is viewed by Okonkwo, and indeed others, as a failure in 'manliness'. Unoka is lazy, and in an agrarian society such as the Ibo's, laziness means poverty. Unoka is also a great debtor. The exchange between him and his friend Okoye in Chapter 1 demonstrates the extent of his debt, but it also gives us a glimpse into a different side of Unoka's personality. He is a spirited conversationalist, a lover of company and talk. He is a musician, and in this brief chapter we come away with the impression that music was the great love of Unoka's life, not just because it appeals to the artistic side of his nature, but because it is the most social of art forms. Unoka is clearly a more complex character than Okonkwo can understand. Of most importance is the fact that Okonkwo's indiscriminate hatred for *all* aspects of his father's personality, the good and the bad, signal the deeper flaws in his own.

Nwoye

Key quotes

'[Okonkwo] sought to correct him by constant nagging and beating. And so Nwoye was developing into a sad-faced youth.' (p.13)

'[Ikemefuna] was like an elder brother to Nwoye, and from the very first seemed to have kindled a new fire in the younger boy.' (p.49)

'It was not the mad logic of the Trinity that captivated him … It was the poetry of the new religion, something felt in the marrow.' (p.139)

Okonkwo's firstborn son, Nwoye, is highly criticised by his father for resembling his grandfather too much. Okonkwo judges him soft and lazy, though there is no real evidence for the latter opinion. Without question, Nwoye is very sensitive; a lover of the folk stories his mother tells, he is repulsed by the so-called 'manly' stories of war and killing to which his father subjects him. Nwoye is filled with troubling questions about life and Ibo practices. The anguish and feelings of deep emptiness he experiences upon hearing the cries of twin babies abandoned in the Evil Forest create in Nwoye a need for guidance that his cruel and unimaginative father cannot fill. For a while Ikemefuna fills the role of guide and counsellor. But following Ikemefuna's murder, Nwoye shrinks farther away from the world of his father and deeper into doubt.

Key point

It is not surprising that Nwoye should convert to Christianity so freely. The new religion seems at least to address the questions disturbing him. However, note that it is less the 'message' of Christianity that attracts him than its 'poetry' and its undertones of fraternity. Though Okonkwo tries to turn Nwoye into a 'man' like himself, it is those characteristics his son shares with Unoka – imagination, sensitivity and sociability – that drive him away.

Ikemefuna

Key quotes

> 'And that was how [Okonkwo] came to look after the doomed lad who was sacrificed to the village of Umuofia ... The ill-fated lad was called Ikemefuna.' (p.8)
>
> 'Although he had felt uneasy at first, he was not afraid now. Okonkwo walked behind him. He could hardly imagine that Okonkwo was not his real father.' (p.56)
>
> '[Okonkwo] heard Ikemefuna cry, "My father, they have killed me!"' (p.57)

The most pitiable figure in *Things Fall Apart* is Ikemefuna, the boy taken from his home without warning and made to live in a new village. The reader first experiences this character through his feelings of absolute fear, confusion and isolation. But he is resourceful and imaginative. He adjusts to life in Umuofia, and soon he is the favourite of Okonkwo's compound. With his store of folk stories, his knowledge of the birds and animals, and his kindness, Ikemefuna wins over Nwoye immediately. The latter sees him as a 'big brother' and guide in life, something he desperately needs.

The order for Ikemefuna's death comes out of nowhere, during a time of the unexpected bounty of a locust plague. This order, in its arbitrariness, reminds us that Ikemefuna's life was never his; it is a possession of the tribe in recompense for one of their own who was murdered. Okonkwo's involvement in the killing tells us something about his character, and indeed, it seems to signal the beginning of Okonkwo's 'downfall'. In some respects it further isolates him from the rest of Umuofia.

Many of the 'little stories' within Achebe's novel seem to be attached to the main story of Okonkwo for anthropological reasons. That is, one of Achebe's goals is to present as many different aspects of Ibo culture as possible *while* telling a compelling story. However, Ikemefuna's sad story seems more than just an 'attached' tale to inform us about certain features of the culture (namely, that a person can be 'ransomed' as payment for a lost life, and that this person can be killed under the order of Agbala).

Key point

The story of the boy taken from his tribe and thrust into a new world – who faces fear and uncertainty in himself and arbitrary cruelty from his new masters – can be considered an allegory for the experience of the Ibo themselves under the power of the British colonisers towards the end of the book.

Ekwefi

Key quotes

'Ekwefi had suffered a good deal in her life.' (p.72)

'Ekwefi believed deep inside her that Ezinma had come to stay. She believed because it was that faith alone that gave her own life any kind of meaning.' (p.76)

Ekwefi was known as the village beauty when she was young. In love with the great wrestler and warrior Okonkwo, she could not marry him because he had not yet made his fortune. Once this occurred, she ran away from her husband to become Okonkwo's second wife. Her life since then has been marked by tragedy. Nine of her children died in infancy or very early childhood. It is determined that she has been giving birth to the same child – an *ogbanje* (changeling).

Ekwefi's fate has left her isolated among Okonkwo's other wives and the women of Umuofia. She is seen as envious of and bitter towards those who have been able to produce many children (in Ibo society a woman's worth is judged by her ability to produce and raise children). In addition, her life with Okonkwo has not lived up to the romantic promise of its inception. She is the wife who is beaten and shot at before the Feast of the New Yam. It is no wonder that Ekwefi is so attached to Ezinma, the one daughter who looks as though she may survive. Her anxiety about Ezinma's illness and during the disturbing incident involving Chielo, the priestess of Agbala, gives us a glimpse into the kind of tenderness and family attachment that is not within Okonkwo's capacities. Ekwefi's story also serves as a vehicle through which Achebe can explore the domestic realm of the Ibo.

Ezinma

Key quotes

> 'But it was impossible to refuse Ezinma anything.' (p.72)
>
> '[Okonkwo] never stopped regretting that Ezinma was a girl. Of all his children she alone understood his every mood.' (p.162)

The daughter of Ekwefi and Okonkwo, this girl is deemed to be an *ogbanje* (changeling), 'one of those wicked children who, when they died, entered their mothers' wombs to be born again' (p.73). She is sickly as a young child, but as her health improves, she turns out to be intelligent and mischievous. The wild goose chase on which she leads the medicine man Okagbue in search of her *iyi-uwa* is a good example. Ekwefi and Ezinma have a relationship more like one between equal adults than mother and daughter. She is also Okonkwo's favourite child. He sees that Ezinma understands him better than any of his other children, and so he blames fate for making her a girl – and essentially worthless to him.

Obierika

Key quotes

> 'What you have done will not please the Earth. It is the kind of action for which the goddess wipes out whole families.' (Obierika, pp.62–3)
>
> 'But if the Oracle said that my son should be killed I would neither dispute it nor be the one to do it.' (Obierika, p.63)
>
> 'The white man is very clever. He came quietly and peaceably with his religion … [Now] our clan can no longer act like one. He has put a knife on the things that held us together and we have fallen apart.' (Obierika, p.166)

Okonkwo's closest friend in the tribe, Obierika, is a foil for Okonkwo. In their discussions, Obierika draws out Okonkwo's opinions on certain subjects, primarily because Obierika mostly takes the opposite position. Obierika is a much deeper thinker than his friend. Like Nwoye, he is troubled by the practice of leaving twins in the Evil Forest. He does not participate in the killing of Ikemefuna, and he chastises Okonkwo for doing so. Still, he is a true friend to Okonkwo, managing his farm and finances while Okonkwo serves his seven years of exile in Mbanto. Note his stirring words to the District Commissioner upon the death of Okonkwo: 'That man was one of the greatest men in Umuofia. You drove him to kill himself; and now he will be buried like a dog' (p.197).

It is through Obierika's thoughts that Achebe most eloquently approaches the subject of the effects of the British missionaries on the Ibo people.

Chielo

Key quote

> 'But at that very moment Chielo's voice rose again in her possessed chanting, and Ekwefi recoiled, because there was no humanity there. It was not the same Chielo who sat with her in the market ... It was a different woman – the priestess of Agbala, the Oracle of the Hills and Caves.' (p.101)

This character embodies the persistent duality in Ibo society of the sacred and the secular. Beneath the mundane events of village life is a complex spirit world to which these events are connected. Normally Chielo is just another one of the women of the village – a friend to Ekwefi who calls Ezinma her 'daughter' (p.101). At times, however, she takes on an incredible spiritual power as the priestess of Agbala. During one such time she takes sickly Ezinma miles away from her warm bed to an unknown ceremony inside the shrine of the Oracle of the Hills and Caves. Remember that it is Agbala who calls for the death of Ikemefuna, and so it must have been Chielo, again under the control of the spirit, who conveyed the order.

Uchendu

Key quote

> 'Your mother is there to protect you ... And that is why we say that mother is supreme.' (p.126)

Okonkwo's mother's brother, Uchendu represents the 'maternal' to Okonkwo when he seeks shelter in Mbanto during the years of his exile. Uchendu is old and opinionated. While very few people can tell Okonkwo what to do in Umuofia, he is very much subordinate to Uchendu in Mbanta. In the wisdom of his words about family and kinsmen, Uchendu represents the old ways of the Ibo culture, which are fading due to the influence of the British.

Mr Brown and Mr Smith

Key quotes

> 'And so Mr Brown came to be respected even by the clan, because he trod softly on its faith.' (p.168)
>
> 'Mr Brown learnt a good deal about the religion of the clan and he came to the conclusion that a frontal attack on it would not succeed.' (p.170)
>
> 'Mr Brown's successor was the Reverend James Smith, and he was a different kind of man ... He saw things as black and white. And black was evil.' (p.174)

It is difficult not to think of these two white missionaries to Umuofia as a matched set, different in personality and temperament as they are. Indeed, through their different approaches the pair resembles a good cop / bad cop duo. Mr Brown, the one who listens to the Ibo and who is able to discuss comparative religions with Akunna, is obviously the good cop. The wrathful Smith, spouting his dogma about the 'seeds sown on rocky soil' (p.174), plays the bad cop. But no matter which face the missionary wears, in the long run the result is the same to the Ibo. Brown and Smith are working for the same cause: the total conversion and 'pacification' (to use the District Commissioner's term) of the Ibo people. Smith's approach is more aggressive, and his provocative technique escalates the inevitable conflict, but his difference from Brown is one of degree. Brown does not come away from his discussion with Akunna with a new appreciation for the richness of Ibo religion; he merely concludes that achieving its destruction will require more subtle means than he had thought.

The District Commissioner

Key quotes

'We have a court of law where we judge cases and administer justice just as it is done in my own country ...' (p.184)

'In the many years in which he had toiled to bring civilization to different parts of Africa he had learnt a number of things.' (p.197)

'The story of this man who had killed a messenger and hanged himself would make interesting reading.' (p.197)

This man is not given a name, and this is deliberate on Achebe's part, because he represents the face of British colonialism rather than the opinions of a particular person. He is the perfect figure of the condescending authority of the typical colonial administration. Note again the hypocrisy of his speech about the British system of law that has been brought to the Ibo (p.184). He dispenses these words *as* he delivers judgement on the six men who have not received the benefit of a fair trial, representation or adjudication. He allows them to be arrested under false pretences and to be physically abused. We see plainly how arbitrary the power is of this official. His empty speech is not so much intended for his audience as for himself; through it he justifies his own conduct and reassures himself that his version of morality is the right one, thus allowing him (and the colonisers he represents) a clear conscience.

His planned book, *The Pacification of the Primitive Tribes of the Lower Niger*, will be another kind of empty comfort for the conscience of the colonisers. Many such books were written during the periods of Western colonisation in Africa. Posing as objective studies of cultures like the Ibo's, these books were really vast apologies (in this sense the term does not mean 'an apology', it means a defence of a practice – a justification) for colonial rule. The authors describe 'backwards', 'unenlightened' cultures with the kind of scientific precision that is intended to demonstrate the superiority of their own culture. By allowing themselves to think of complex cultures in such terms (by referring to them as 'primitive') these authors became intellectual colonisers of their subjects, as well as physical colonisers. We see something of this in the way the District Commissioner plans to turn the vast, tragic, complicated story of Okonkwo's life into a mere 'reasonable paragraph' (p.197) in his book.

THEMES, IDEAS & VALUES

Dualities and values in the Ibo culture

Achebe's representation of the Ibo culture tends to focus on dualities – such as those between the spiritual and the secular, the man's realm and the woman's realm, and words and action. He shows how the relationships between these opposites do not occur in the same manner as they do in the West; in some cases there is not the clear-cut distinction that Western cultures tend to make. A lot can be learned about the Ibo simply by examining the relationships between these dualities – what they really value, for example, and how these values are expressed in their daily lives.

The spiritual and the secular

Things Fall Apart explores the connection between the spiritual and the secular in Ibo culture: 'The land of the living was not far removed from the domain of the ancestors' (p.115). For example, the funeral of Ezeudu is described by Achebe as a high-pitched, nearly hysterical affair encompassing the entire clan – not just the living members, but also the spirits of the ancestors, as represented by the *egwugwu*. On occasions such as the funeral of an old man – 'because an old man was very close to the ancestors' (p.115) – or festivals, the borders between the spiritual world and the everyday world are removed: 'there was coming and going between them' (p.115). During the funeral, the *egwugwu* seem to be serving at least one important function – that of welcoming the soul of Ezeudu to the ancestors. Otherwise, they seem to take part in the chaotic proceedings just as any other living mourners do. This underscores the fact that the *egwugwu* really are a vital part of everyday life in the village. They are members of the clan who simply do not happen to be living.

The part the *egwugwu* play in adjudicating important civil disputes (as in Chapter 10) also clearly shows how the secular and spiritual worlds of the Ibo are aligned. Indeed, without the intervention of the spirit world, the secular world could not function – there would be no civil authority and no coherence. Ibo law seems to be directed entirely by the will of the spirits, as voiced by ancestors in the form of the *egwugwu*, or by the Oracle of the Hills and Caves, or by the doctrines handed down from the past (under some assumed spiritual direction). The spirits take part in everything – when the crop shall be planted, when the festivals shall occur, even down to very mundane subjects such as who shall be allowed to tap the tall palm trees for palm wine.

Key point

For the Ibo, we see that there really is very little division between the spiritual and the secular worlds; the spirits are part of every aspect of life. This is quite different from the role religion plays in the West. Notice the approach of the English missionaries, who build themselves a separate place and set aside one of the seven days of their week specifically for worship. The fact that the civil authority for the missionaries is totally secular (in the person of the District Commissioner) would highlight for the Ibo just how defined the borders are between 'the land of the living' and the world of the spirits for these new 'neighbours'.

Spiritual and secular 'personalities'

The close relationship between the spiritual and the secular in the Ibo culture can be seen in multiple characters in *Things Fall Apart*. Think of Chielo, the priestess of Agbala. Here there is a strong duality: Chielo is essentially two different people. The ordinary woman of no particular standing in the tribe becomes, at the time of her possession by the spirit of the Oracle, a powerful entity dictating law that no-one would conceive of disobeying. And there is Ezinma, the *ogbanje*, who, perhaps until her dying day, will be thought of as both the person she is and a mischievous sprite from the other world. There are numerous other examples, including the sacred cotton-silk tree near the *ilo* that is both a tree and the home for the spirits of children that have not yet been born. The fact that the spirit world and the everyday world are so closely aligned allows the Ibo to see a double quality to what we might call the most mundane objects, such as Ezinma's rock (called the *iyi-uwa*) or the cotton-silk tree. (The religious belief that objects possess a distinct spiritual essence is referred to as 'animism'.)

The man's realm and the woman's realm

In Ibo society, there is a very strong contrast between the women's world and the men's world, defined by Uchendu in these terms:

> We all know that a man is the head of the family and his wives do his bidding. A child belongs to its father and his family and not to its mother and her family. A man belongs to his fatherland and not to his motherland. (p.125)

On the other hand, think of Uchendu celebrating the role of the mother in Mbanto, or think of the husband and wife Ndulue and Ozoemena, who die one after the other in old age. It is said of them that they had 'one mind' (p.64). Despite these examples, there is no doubt that Ibo society is patriarchal. The man is the absolute ruler of the compound comprising multiple wives and children. However, there are lines of demarcation between the sexes beyond the hierarchy of power. The rituals that men and women are expected to undertake during the marriage festival, for example, are telling: the men bargain for the bride over palm wine while the women test her skills as a cook.

The crime Okonkwo commits, the killing of one of the mourners at Ezeudu's funeral, is called a 'female' crime because it was accidental; for this reason it carries a lesser punishment than a male crime. We also see how the culture is divided through the kinds of stories men and women tell. In his *obi*, Okonkwo tells Nwoye and Ikemefuna bloodcurdling stories of war and violence in order to wean them off the kind of folktales their mothers have told them since their childhood. Women are keepers of the stories that house the wisdom, and to a large extent the identity, of the clan. It should be noted that many of the other men of the clan use and relish these kind of folktales. When Obierika tells Okonkwo and his uncle about the massacre of Abame, they react in very different ways. Okonkwo calls the men of Abame fools for not being better prepared for war; Uchendu calls them fools for not heeding the advice from one of the best-known Ibo folktales about Kite and her daughter.

Again, we cannot judge the Ibo as a whole by Okonkwo's opinions. He is in many ways a backward and ignorant man, nowhere more so than in his opinions on women. Still, while there are men like Ndulue, who are willing to treat their wives as equals, there are also men like Okonkwo and Uzowulu (whose case the *egwugwu* decide in Chapter 10), who beat their wives (even to death) if they see fit. Such sexism can arise at least in part from the very strict duality between the sexes that the Ibo culture maintains.

Words and actions

There is a duality between speech and deeds among the Ibo. In this they are not different from the rest of the world, but perhaps they are more extreme. The Ibo hold public or ritualised speaking in very high regard. Interestingly, the incidence of stammering (remember, Okonkwo stammers) is five times higher among the Ibo than around the world. It is thought that the high standards by which speakers are judged and the nervousness this creates are responsible.

In Chapter 24, Okonkwo imagines the speeches that will be made the next morning at the council of men in Umuofia. He longs for the kind of speeches once made by Okudo and reviles the kind he expects will come from Egonwanne. When a man can speak well (Okudo), it is not necessary that he be a good fighter. Okonkwo is very uncomfortable speaking, but he too makes a studied speech when he comes to Nwakibie to ask for his help in starting a farm for himself. However, later in life Okonkwo dispenses with speech whenever he can. He wants his deeds to do his speaking for him. The Ibo believe very strongly in actions too, but there is some indication that his clansmen see Okonkwo as carrying this a little too far, most notably in his taking part in the killing of Ikemefuna.

The irony in some of Okonkwo's actions throughout the novel speak to the duality between words and actions. Some of these actions are performed for the sole reason of not wanting to appear weak and thus alienating himself from the men of the clan. But these actions alienate him in a different way; they show him to be hard, cold and uncaring. This is true not only in the killing of Ikemefuna. After Okonkwo breaks the rules of the Week of Peace, he feels genuine contrition (not for beating Ojiugo, but for offending the gods). But he does not admit it for fear of appearing weak to his neighbours. The result is that he appears to them as something far worse – a man who does not respect the gods of the clan, who has let success go to his head. In the terms of Greek tragedy, Okonkwo is being accused of showing hubris (the pride and ambition that makes one challenge one's assigned fate).

Again, in downplaying the importance of speech and choosing to express himself through action, Okonkwo drives a wedge between himself and the rest of his clan. This is most evident in the penultimate chapter, which highlights the irony in Okonkwo killing the messenger during the speeches made by the other men, without uttering a word himself. And remember, it is through the words of the other men (asking why he did it) that he realises they will not follow the lead of his actions. Though he does not say so explicitly, Okonkwo would have believed that the formerly brave and noble men of Umuofia had been bewitched by words – the soothing and inviting words of the Christians – to betray themselves and their identities. This is exactly what he has seen happen to his eldest son, Nwoye.

Postcolonial issues

Cultural 'superiority' and dominance over another culture

A central issue in postcolonial texts is the dominance of one culture over another. This dominance is not just limited to military or even political advantage. Rather, full hegemony (defined as 'leadership, authority or influence') involves controlling and changing the indigenous culture itself – the religion, law, rituals, education system and language – into mirror images of the corresponding institutions of the coloniser. The British were particularly interested in this form of colonisation, perhaps more so than other European colonialist nations. The way they saw it – at least when they were trying to rationalise the practice of colonialism and the enormous wealth it brought them – was that they had a responsibility to 'improve' the lives of those people who were coming under their control. Much of this has to do with their particularly Victorian-era form of morality – some would call it hypocrisy bred of extreme prejudice. On the one hand, this form of morality could not allow one to pass by those in need, and on the other hand it could not allow for the idea that people in a culture different from Britain's were not in need of assistance.

How you view the situation depends on how you look at the issue. The British claimed that they were bringing civilisation to nations that *also* happened to offer the possibility of enormous wealth. Others would conclude that the British, not content with ransacking a nation's treasures and natural resources, also wanted to steal the identity, indeed, the very souls of its people. Either way, without question, the issue is one of cultural superiority. The British were famous for their diligence in studying the cultures of their colonised subjects, but this acquired knowledge did nothing to shift their view that these cultures were inherently inferior to their own.

British systems – the legacy of colonialism

One of the reasons that most postcolonial literature is written in English has to do with the legacy of the British form of colonialism. Long after the British have left the nations they once controlled, the systems they put in place – the religion, the education system, the language – have remained. Now, in this regard there is not much difference between the former British colonies and those of, say, France or Spain. However, something about the way the British tried to change the *whole* society and culture, to turn the peoples themselves into quasi-Britons, created a debilitating sense of 'in-betweenness' in those colonised nations.

Postcolonial literature was created by the generations of people who felt lost somewhere 'in between' cultures; they were not Britons, but the connections they had to their own cultural past had been cut. These writers, recognising just how insidious this form of colonialism was, set out to study the complex colonial world and try to represent it from the perspective of the colonised people by sharing their experiences.

Change in the Ibo culture

Achebe's intention as a writer was to present colonialism from the perspective of his own people. While *Things Fall Apart* looks only at the period when the British first came into contact with the Ibo, his other books have examined different stages in the colonial relationship. *Things Fall Apart* is most interested (in its postcolonial aspect) in describing how the British initiated their quest for dominance over the Ibo. Their strategy is addressed in Obierika's assessment of the arrival of the white man:

> The white man is very clever. He came quietly and peaceably with his religion. We were amused at his foolishness and allowed him to stay. Now he has won our brothers, and our clan can no longer act like one. He has put a knife on the things that held us together and we have fallen apart. (p.166)

Changing religious beliefs and achieving power over the Ibo

How did the British bring about change and achieve their dominance over the Ibo? The missionaries came first. In a sense, they 'softened up' the Ibo by winning some converts where they could. Remember, the first converts were not just men that the clan thought of as *efulefu* (worthless); the new religion also appealed to those people left out of Ibo society, the *osu*, or those like Nneka, whose children had been left to die in the Evil Forest. Once members of the clan convert, the strength and unity of the clan is undermined. There can no longer be any question of killing the missionaries and the converts or of driving them out. The particularly insidious thing about this strategy is that while it is the strong bonds of kinship that protect the young church, these bonds are the very things it is intent on destroying in the Ibo culture. While Mr Brown wins a favourable name for himself among the Ibo because 'he trod softly on its faith' (p.168), his primary intention is to destroy the religion of the

Ibo and convert the population to Christianity. Think again of the speech that the chief of the *egwugwu* makes to Mr Smith before the burning of the church: 'You can worship your own god. It is good that a man should worship the gods and the spirits of his fathers' (p.180). The Christianity as practised by these missionaries has nothing of the Ibo tolerance for other religions.

Imposing foreign law – undermining Ibo authority

Once the Ibo have been 'softened up' and divided by religion, the civil authority moves in to impose foreign law on them. While the District Commissioner's form of law only remotely resembles the British law it professes to be, the Ibo see it as corrupt and arbitrary, and would no doubt do so even if the District Commissioner correctly administered British law. The new form of law further breaks the bond of the clan by destroying the authority of the *egwugwu*. One can imagine that it will not be very long before the terror and awe the Ibo feel at the sight of these representatives of the ancestors will disappear entirely. The British would see this as a beneficial quelling of naive superstition, a step in the right direction. For the Ibo it means another wedge driven between themselves and the spirits of their gods. Achebe alludes to the effect of this division in the following passage:

> [Okonkwo] saw himself and his father crowding round their ancestral shrine waiting in vain for worship and sacrifice and finding nothing but ashes of bygone days, and his children the while praying to the white man's god. (pp.144–5)

Introducing new forms of trade

Not long after a civil authority has been established, trade really begins to pick up in Umuofia. This is one of the primary reasons why some of the Ibo begin to look more favourably on the British; there is money to be made. Of course this is a relatively new form of commerce, one that has very little to do with the traditions of the Ibo. As they are tempted to leave their old practices, the Ibo will become more and more dependent, part of an introduced economy detached from their traditional ways. The Ibo also look favourably on the new medicines brought by the British (there is no mention made in *Things Fall Apart* of the diseases the British also brought with them, against which these medicines were largely powerless). This is another step in complete dominance of the Ibo, as it makes them dependent on the colonising culture.

Changing education and language

The most powerful tool in bringing about change and increasing the colonisers' dominance is something that Mr Brown introduces: the school. Note how Mr Brown begins to urge the Ibo to send their children to the British school after he realises that their religion will not succumb to a 'frontal attack' (p.170). He knows that colonialism is a long-term project, and that if you cannot win over the present generation you need to focus on the next. The school intends to do just that.

So much of the identity of a person is determined by their education. As the succeeding generations of Ibo are sent to the British school, the things taught to them there will become the 'standard' in their lives, the foundation of their thinking. Ibo culture will become secondary, even if some of the Ibo want to preserve their culture. As the British way becomes standard, the Ibo culture will fall into disrepute; it will come to be considered inferior. It is likely that the generations educated by the British will lose their connection with their culture except for a few vestiges.

In addition, at school Ibo children will learn English, the language of the colonisers. This will also become the language of their new religion, of commerce and trade, and of law, history and literature – as taught at these new institutions. The Ibo language will inevitably assume second-class status. It may not disappear entirely, but it will become almost foreign to the younger generations. Their direct connection to it will be cut, and with it their strongest tie to their law, their history, their literature – their culture.

Achebe's representation of pre-British Ibo culture

Achebe's novel is a multi-faceted jewel. One should look closely at what *Things Fall Apart* has to say about Ibo culture as it existed *before* being tainted by the British. Achebe is by no means uncritical. Like his characters Obierika and Nwoye, Achebe seems to be very troubled by such practices as leaving the twins to die in the Evil Forest. He questions aspects of a culture that would allow the boy Ikemefuna to be killed because of the word of the Oracle. Likewise, he seems to be deeply troubled by the tradition of the *osu*, the caste of untouchables. In other words, he presents the Ibo 'warts and all'. Neither entirely complimentary nor dismissive of the Ibo culture, Achebe tries to give us the whole picture as he sees it. And this is the way that he gives his culture back its 'voice'. This simply could not be done in a treatment that was sentimental and uncritical. One cannot analyse colonialism by adopting, in reverse, one of its practices: the misrepresentation of the culture of the colonised subject.

Thus Achebe's novel is most characteristically postcolonial in these two aspects: its description of the early stages of Britain's attempts to gain dominance over the cultures of Nigeria; and the full and fair presentation of the Ibo. He lets the Ibo speak for themselves, something that colonisers traditionally never allow the colonised subject to do.

QUESTIONS & ANSWERS

This section focuses on your own analytical writing on the text, and gives you strategies for producing high-quality responses in your coursework and exam essays.

Essay writing – an overview

An essay on a literary work is a formal and serious piece of writing that presents your point of view on the text, usually in response to a given topic. Your 'point of view' in an essay is your interpretation of the meaning of the text's language, structure, characters, situations and events, supported by detailed analysis of textual evidence.

Analyse – don't summarise

In your essays it is important to avoid simply summarising what happens in a text.

- A **summary** is a description or paraphrase (retelling in different words) of the characters and events. For example: 'Macbeth has a horrifying vision of a dagger dripping with blood before he goes to murder King Duncan.'
- An **analysis** is an explanation of the real meaning or significance that lies 'beneath' the text's words (and images, for a film). For example: 'Macbeth's vision of a bloody dagger shows how deeply uneasy he is about the violent act he is contemplating, and conveys his sense that supernatural forces are impelling him to act.'

A limited amount of summary is sometimes necessary to let your reader know which part of the text you wish to discuss. However, always keep this to a minimum and follow it immediately with your analysis of what this part of the text is really telling us.

Plan your essay

Carefully plan your essay so that you have a clear idea of what you are going to say. The plan ensures that your ideas flow logically, that your argument remains consistent and that you stay on the topic. An essay plan should be a list of **brief dot points** covering no more than half a page.

- Include your central argument or main contention – a concise statement of your overall response to the topic.
- Write three or four dot points for each paragraph, indicating the main idea and evidence/examples from the text. Note that in your essay you will need to *expand* on these points and *analyse* the evidence.

Structure your essay

An essay is a complete, self-contained piece of writing. It has a clear beginning (the introduction), middle (several body paragraphs) and end (the last paragraph or conclusion). It must also have a central argument that runs throughout, linking each paragraph to form a coherent whole. See examples of an introduction and a conclusion in the 'Sample answer' section.

The introduction establishes your overall response to the topic. It includes your main contention and outlines the main evidence you will refer to in the course of the essay. Write your introduction *after* you have done a plan and *before* you write the rest of the essay.

The body paragraphs argue your case – they present evidence from the text and explain how this evidence supports your argument. Each body paragraph needs:

- a strong **topic sentence** (usually the first sentence) that states the main point being made in the paragraph
- **evidence** from the text, including some brief quotations
- **analysis** of the textual evidence, with **explanation** of its significance and how it supports your argument
- **links back to the topic** in one or more statements, usually towards the end of the paragraph.

Connect the body paragraphs so that your discussion flows smoothly. Use some linking words and phrases such as 'similarly' and 'on the other hand', though don't start every paragraph like this. Another strategy is to use a significant word from the last sentence of one paragraph in the first sentence of the next.

Use key terms from the topic – or synonyms for them – throughout, so the relevance of your discussion to the topic is always clear.

The conclusion ties everything together and finishes the essay. It includes strong statements that emphasise your central argument and provide a clear response to the topic.

Avoid simply restating the points made earlier in the essay – this will end on a very flat note and imply that you have run out of ideas and vocabulary. The conclusion should be a logical extension of what you have written, not just a repetition or summary of it. Writing an effective conclusion can be a challenge. Try using these tips:

- Start by linking back to the final sentence of the second-last paragraph – this helps your writing to flow, rather than leaping back to your main contention straight away.
- Use synonyms and expressions with equivalent meanings to vary your vocabulary. This allows you to reinforce your line of argument without being repetitive.
- When planning your essay, think of one or two broad statements or observations about the text's wider meaning. These should be related to the topic and your overall argument. Keep them for the conclusion, since they will give you something 'new' to say but still follow logically from your discussion. The introduction will be focused on the topic, but the conclusion can present a wider view of the text.

Essay topics

1. In what ways is Okonkwo a tragic hero?
2. '*Things Fall Apart* is a postcolonial text because it gives a voice to the voiceless.'
   Discuss.
3. 'Okonkwo represents the best and worst of his culture.'
   To what extent do you agree?
4. '*Things Fall Apart* shows that Ibo culture is dominated by men and their actions.'
   Discuss.
5. "What you have done will not please the Earth. It is the kind of action for which the goddess wipes out whole families."
   What role does fate play in Okonkwo's story?
6. "It was not the mad logic of the Trinity that captivated him …
   It was the poetry of the new religion."
   What role does religion play in *Things Fall Apart*?
7. '*Things Fall Apart* shows how the British undermine Ibo culture.'
   Discuss.
8. "Among the Ibo the art of conversation is regarded very highly …"
   How does Achebe explore the importance of story to the Ibo?
9. In your view, does Achebe invite the reader to judge and condemn the British colonisers?
10. What makes 'things fall apart' in Achebe's text?

Analysing a sample topic

This section leads you through the analysis of a topic and the planning of a response.

"The question of the twins crying in the bush and the question of Ikemefuna who was killed."
'Achebe's novel does not refrain from presenting the Ibo in a negative light at times.' Discuss.

The question is asking you to discuss a particular strategy the author took in writing his novel. To answer this question, you will need to consider not just this aspect, but Achebe's *overall* intention. The opinion suggested in this guide is that Achebe has written the novel to change the way the world has come to think of native Africans as shown through years of colonial representations. What is it that Achebe wants us to understand about his subjects, the Ibo of Nigeria? To grasp that, you should think about the way colonial literature has represented Africans in the past – as primitive people, as savages, as 'exotics'. Put yourself in Achebe's shoes. How is it best to counter prejudicial opinions about the Ibo? All prejudice relies on oversimplification, on a reduction of an entire people to an uncomplicated, easily digested stereotype. It can be argued that Achebe has determined that the way to combat stereotyping is to show the Ibo as complex, unpredictable and difficult to understand.

Once you have determined how you will approach the topic, you will need to write a contention that clearly states your position.

Consider the evidence that you will use to support your contention. You will need to discuss those situations in which Achebe presents the Ibo in an honest, unsentimental fashion. The question has supplied you with two examples: the twins left in the Evil Forest to die, and the killing of Ikemefuna under the order of the Oracle of the Hills and Caves. Other examples that you may choose to discuss to show a greater understanding of the text are listed on the next page.

- Certain members of the clan of Umuofia (the *osu*) are deemed outcasts for no other reason than that their ancestors were servants of the gods many years earlier.
- Obierika questions why a man like Okonkwo should be punished so severely for a 'female crime', a complete accident (the death of the mourner at the funeral of Ezeudu).
- Unoka is left to die alone and in misery in the Evil Forest because he contracted the 'swelling' disease.
- It is common practice among the Ibo for the men of the clan to beat their wives.

You may conclude that there are a lot of things about Ibo culture that Achebe finds distasteful or wrong; however, it is not enough to focus on these alone. In order to show that Achebe's account of his people is impartial, you will also need to discuss positive aspects of Ibo culture in your response. Some positive examples of Ibo culture that you could include are listed below.

- The Ibo have a rich tradition of telling folktales and participating in festivals and rituals that bring the clan together.
- As an agrarian society, the Ibo take pride in the hard work necessary to yield crops.
- The Ibo are tolerant of other religions, as shown when Ajofia tells Mr Smith, 'You can worship your own god. It is good that a man should worship the gods and the spirits of his fathers' (p.180).

Create a brief outline for yourself ordering the supporting evidence you will use in your argument. Experiment with this order in your outline to come up with the most effective plan.

Remember, while you want to answer the question fully, and while you do not want to stray from the topic, questions such as this are designed to allow you to demonstrate your close knowledge of the text. Show the assessors that you understand the political importance of *Things Fall Apart* in your discussion of why Achebe has shown the Ibo in a negative light at times – that is, he is conscious not to replicate the bias shown by colonisers.

SAMPLE ANSWER

"What you have done will not please the Earth. It is the kind of action for which the goddess wipes out whole families."

What role does fate play in Okonkwo's story?

Achebe never explicitly states in *Things Fall Apart* that there is some kind of supernatural agency directing Okonkwo's life. To do so would be to step out of the role he has chosen as the chronicler of Okonkwo's story. Achebe reports the events and lets readers make up their own minds – just as he does regarding other aspects of Ibo culture. But the characters in the novel believe very strongly in fate. They call one's personal fate *chi*, and Okonkwo is constantly worried about what his *chi* may have in store for him. He alternates between feeling that a strong man like himself can influence his *chi* and feeling entirely powerless before it. Enough 'fateful' events occur to make him feel as though his life is being controlled by some outside force, and, ultimately, a reading of Achebe's novel would suggest that fate – or what the Ibo perceive to be the work of the gods – plays a significant role in Okonkwo's downfall.

While the Ibo believe strongly in outside forces affecting their everyday lives, they do not believe that fateful events occur for no reason; in their eyes, these events are caused by offences committed against the gods. This is evident in the case of Okonkwo, who acts against the gods several times before his banishment from the tribe. The first instance of this in the novel is when he violates the Week of Peace by beating his wife Ojiugo. Not only does Okonkwo commit a crime insulting the gods, but he also fails to show the proper shame for what he has done from fear of looking weak: 'Inwardly, he was repentant. But he was not the man to go about telling his neighbours that he was in error. And so people said he had no respect for the gods of the clan'. Here, Okonkwo's desire to appear strong undermines the respect he is required to exhibit to the gods. This character flaw is also on display when Okonkwo takes part in the killing of Ikemefuna, after which Obierika tells him: 'What you have done will not please the Earth. It is the kind of action for which the goddess wipes out whole families.' Obierika believes, as do other elders of the tribe, that Okonkwo was wrong to take part in the death of one who 'calls him father'. The events that befall Okonkwo following these indiscretions can be regarded as a direct result of his own actions in provoking the wrath of the gods.

The role played by Okonkwo in the murder of Ikemefuna, a boy who thought of him as his father, as well as his earlier indiscretions against the gods has repercussions for both Okonkwo and his family. It is interesting that the Oracle comes for Okonkwo's favourite child, Ezinma, very soon after the killing of Ikemefuna. While his daughter is returned safely to her mother, she and Okonkwo receive a terrible scare. This could be interpreted as a kind of warning or minor punishment from the goddess Agbala for Okonkwo's role in the death of Ikemefuna. But the event that most clearly draws a line between Okonkwo's actions and retribution by the gods, and the one that most strongly affects the life of Okonkwo's family, is the accidental killing of one of the mourners at Ezeudu's funeral. It is important to note that the gun that kills the mourner is the same one with which Okonkwo had unsuccessfully tried to kill his wife Ekwefi. It was only the gun's misfiring that had saved Ekwefi on that occasion. In this way, Okonkwo's misfortune seems fitting, as though it were indeed punishment for a previous transgression. As suggested, the price the family pays is great: they have to endure seven years of exile from Umuofia. But for Okonkwo it is even greater, as it means that he has to give up all his ambitions for becoming the leader of the tribe.

The punishment exacted on Okonkwo by the gods is not only an assault on his everyday life, but also on his spiritual connection to the Ibo culture. This is manifested through the loss of his eldest son, Nwoye, to the new religion brought by the British missionaries. Okonkwo has turned his son away from him with his own violence and brutality, but he does not recognise this, blaming the loss on his *chi*. Again, it can be argued that, if indeed it is due to fate, the loss of Nwoye is the compensation taken by the gods for Okonkwo's role in the killing of Ikemefuna. This is particularly poignant given Nwoye's close relationship with Ikemefuna, who 'was like an elder brother to Nwoye'. Upon learning of his father's role in Ikemefuna's murder, Nwoye feels that 'something seemed to give way inside him'. The profound effect of this event on Nwoye and his psychological wellbeing makes him more susceptible to the missionaries' attempts to convert him to Christianity, which he eventually comes to see as an answer to 'a vague and persistent question that haunted his young soul – the question of the twins crying in the bush and the question of Ikemefuna who was killed'. Thus, Okonkwo's failure to adhere to the gods' wishes sees him lose his eldest son, who comes to represent the loss of the Ibo culture to British colonisers.

Throughout *Things Fall Apart*, the influence of fate on the protagonist's life is shown to be potent and far-reaching. Through his callous and cruel actions, Okonkwo incurs the wrath of the gods. His subsequent demise can be read as the result of their interference, which Obierika warns him will happen – advice that Okonkwo wilfully chooses to ignore. In the end, the gods play a notable role in making 'things fall apart' for Okonkwo.

REFERENCES & READING

The text

Achebe, C 2006, *Things Fall Apart*, Penguin, London. First published in 1958.

Interviews with the author

Bacon, K 2000, 'An African Voice', *The Atlantic Monthly*, August, https://www.theatlantic.com/magazine/archive/2000/08/an-african-voice/306020/

Brooks, J 1994, 'Chinua Achebe, The Art of Fiction No. 139', *The Paris Review*, https://www.theparisreview.org/interviews/1720/chinua-achebe-the-art-of-fiction-no-139-chinua-achebe

Books

Afigbo, A 1981, *Ropes of Sand: Studies in Igbo History and Culture*, Oxford University Press, Ibadan.

Amuta, C 1989, *The Theory of African Literature: Implications for Practical Criticism*, Zed Books, London.

Ashcroft, B, Griffiths, G & Tiffin, H 1989, *The Empire Writes Back: Theory and Practice in Post-Colonial Literatures*, Routledge, London.

Booker, M 1998, *The African Novel in English: An Introduction, Studies in African Literature*, Heinemann, Oxford.

Carroll, D 1980, *Chinua Achebe*, Palgrave Macmillan, London.

Gikandi, S 1991, *Reading Chinua Achebe: Language and Ideology in Fiction*, James Currey, Oxford.

Innes, C 1990, *Chinua Achebe: Cambridge Studies in African and Caribbean Literature 1*, Cambridge University Press, Cambridge.

Isichei, E 1976, *A History of the Igbo People,* St. Martin's Press, New York.

Killam, G 1969, *The Writings of Chinua Achebe,* Heinemann, London.

Lindfors, B (ed.) 1991, *Approaches to Teaching Achebe's* Things Fall Apart, Modern Language Association of America, New York.